CULTURES OF THE WORLD®

BRAZIL

Christopher Richard & Leslie Jermyn

MARSHALL CAVENDISH BENCHMARK

NEW YORK

PICTURE CREDITS
Cover photo: © Wolfgang Kaehler
Steve Cohen / Houserstock: 39 • Lupe Cunha Brazil Photo Library: 6, 9 (both), 10, 11, 29, 36, 50, 69, 73, 76, 119, 123, 128 • Bira da Silveira: 120, 127 • Embassy of Brazil in Singapore: 19 • Victor Englebert: 4 (top), 8, 12, 55, 66, 85, 121, 124 • Focus Team: 54, 88, 130 • Eduardo Gil: 18 • S. Gutierrez / ANA Press Agency: 44, 45 • Haga Library Inc.: 110 • Rankin Harvey / Houserstock: 5, 32, 38, 43, 46 • The Hutchison Library: 3, 16, 63, 67, 71, 74, 75, 93, 102, 117 • Abril Imagens: 17, 20, 21, 22, 23, 28, 35, 37, 47, 51, 59, 83, 96 (bottom), 104, 115, 122 • John Maier, Jr.: 1, 4 (bottom), 7, 14, 26, 34, 49, 53, 56, 57, 58, 61, 64, 70, 72, 79, 98, 99, 105, 106, 108, 109, 111 • MC Picture Library: 131 • Chris Richard: 25 • South American Pictures: 13, 15, 33, 78, 80, 82, 94, 95, 96 (top), 97, 107, 112, 113, 114, 126, 129 • Topham Picturepoint: 100 • Trip Photographic Library: 68

ACKNOWLEDGMENTS
With thanks to Delmarie Martinez, Assistant Professor University of Central Florida, for her expert reading of the manuscript.

PRECEDING PAGE
Carnival in Rio de Janeiro.

Marshall Cavendish Benchmark
99 White Plains Road
Tarrytown, NY 10591
Website: www.marshallcavendish.us

© Times Media Private Limited 1990, 2002
© Marshall Cavendish International (Asia) Private Limited 2004
All rights reserved. First edition 1990. Second edition 2002.
® "Cultures of the World" is a registered trademark of Times Publishing Limited.

Originated and designed by Times Editions
An imprint of Marshall Cavendish International (Asia) Private Limited
A member of Times Publishing Limited

All Internet sites were correct and accurate at the time of printing.

Library of Congress Cataloging-in-Publication Data
Richard, Christopher, 1959–
    Brazil / Christopher Richard, Leslie Jermyn. – 2nd ed.
        p. cm. – (Cultures of the world)
        Includes bibliographical references and index.
    Summary: Presents the geography, history, government, economy, and social life and customs of the South
        American country of Brazil, which has the world's longest continuous coastline.
    ISBN 0-7614-1359-6
    1. Brazil—Juvenile literature. [1. Brazil.] I. Jermyn, Leslie. II. Title. III. Series
    F2508.5 .R53 2002
    981—dc21   2001047263

Printed in Malaysia

7 6 5

CONTENTS

A *candomblé* (religion with African roots) procession in the northern city of Salvador.

A Yanomami Indian in the Amazon forest reserve.

Two young Brazilians enjoy a windowside chat.

INTRODUCTION

BRAZIL INSPIRES DIFFERENT IMAGES for different people. Some see one big tropical rain forest filled with curious creatures and raging rivers. Others picture the brilliant sights and sounds of Carnival in Rio. Still others imagine miles of pristine beaches. For a lucky few, Brazil conjures images of a beautiful and friendly people as diverse as the land they inhabit.

Brazil is all of these and more. This is where you'll find the largest variety of species in any nation in the world. This is the home of some of the world's greatest soccer players and the only country to have won the World Cup four times. This is where African and European cultures and religions blend in harmony. This is the home of a dazzling array of music and dance styles and some of the most remarkable artists in the Western Hemisphere. Brazil is also an industrial and economic powerhouse that has risen from being just another Third World country to being a major international force. In short, Brazil holds something for everyone.

GEOGRAPHY

BRAZIL IS THE FIFTH LARGEST and sixth most populous nation in the world. Covering almost half of South America's land area, the country is as large as the whole of Europe. It is so vast that it borders every South American country except Chile and Ecuador and has the world's longest continuous coastline. Brazil's easternmost piece of land is closer to Africa than to its southern border with Uruguay. A traveler on a ship several miles up the Amazon River would have a hard time distinguishing the river from the ocean. The mouth of the Amazon River is 200 miles (322 km) wide; at some points 1,000 miles (1,609 km) inland, the river is seven miles (11 km) across.

The equator runs across the north of Brazil, and 90 percent of the country lies in the tropical zone. However, as most of Brazil lies 2,000 feet (610 m) above sea level, the landscape is not all tropical. While the Amazon basin is covered in tropical rain forest, the central area is mainly savanna with sparse vegetation. One-fourth of all known plant species and a third of all iron ore reserves are found in Brazil.

The country can be divided into three regions: the north and central-west have few people but great economic potential; the northeast is rich in history but poor in economy; and the southeast and south are home to most of the population and wealth.

Waters of the Rio Negro, one of the Amazon's tributaries, mirror the jungle at dusk.

THE AMAZON

Covering 40 percent of Brazil's land area in the north, the vast Amazon is the world's largest river basin and tropical rain forest. Scientists believe that the Amazon River and jungle produce one-third of the world's oxygen and hold one-fifth of its freshwater resources.

The Amazon River is fed by a vast system of tributaries, 17 of which are over 1,000 miles (1,609 km) long. It is the second longest river in the world: 3,990 miles (6,421 km) from where it starts in the Andes Mountains to where it drains into the Atlantic Ocean. Every second, it sends 80 million gallons (303 million liters) of water into the Atlantic Ocean—more than the output of the next three biggest rivers in the world put together. The Amazon receives water from the Andes Mountains in the west, the Guyana Highlands in the north, and Brazil's Central Plateau in the south. The river drains an area almost the size of Australia.

The Amazonian jungle, which covers most of this basin, makes up one-third of the world's natural forests. Over the years, its mystery has attracted countless explorers. The Spaniards searched it for the mythical El Dorado

MIRACLE PLANTS

The first explorers who crossed the Andes Mountains found Indians using a white crystal extracted from the bark of the *cinchona* ("sin-SHOH-nah") tree as medicine. Hundreds of years later, scientists discovered that this crystal, called quinine, effectively protects people from the tropical disease of malaria.

Today, scientists called ethnobotanists believe that plants in the Amazon might hold a cure for Acquired Immune Deficiency Syndrome (AIDS), leukemia, and cancer. They believe that the disappearing rain forests and the Indians who live in them should be protected, for they hold secrets which "civilized" people have yet to learn.

Ethnobotanists depend on the Indians' knowledge of the jungle just as much as they depend on chemistry or biology. There are already examples of indigenous medicines in use: street vendors in Manaus, the capital of the state of Amazonas, peddle various plants as cures for problems ranging from head lice to swollen intestines.

Scientists are now exploring the jungle with Indian medicine men and observing the way they put plants to use: how a liquid squeezed from a fungus growing on dead trees can be used to treat earaches or tea made from a red berry can be used to fight fevers. With the richness of the Amazon's biodiversity, perhaps one day ethnobotanists will discover more medicinal cures for some of the world's most serious illnesses.

Below: **Anteaters capable of growing to five feet (1.5 m) in length sniff and snuff out anthills in the Amazon.**

Bottom: **The capybara, the world's largest rodent, weighs some 150 pounds (68 kg).**

400 years ago. The Spaniards also created another myth, that of a fierce group of women warriors called Amazons, which gave the area its name. Today explorers in the Amazon still find Indians who have never met an outsider, and scientists there still discover new kinds of insects and animals. Botanists believe that the 25,000 plants cataloged represent only half of the jungle's total plant population. Trees 200 feet (61 m) high form a continuous canopy, blocking out almost all sunlight from the forest floor. Rivers crisscross the area, and tropical storms frequently cause flooding.

Countless strange creatures exist among the Amazon's 10,000 known species, such as howler monkeys, whose screams can be heard miles away, and ant armies that devour plants and animals in their path.

Brasília, the nation's capital, captured the world's imagination during its construction in the 1950s.

THE CENTRAL-WEST

The central-west contains four states and the Federal District of Brasília. With about 2 million residents, the Federal District has a population larger than three of the region's four states. The government built Brasília from scratch and made it the nation's capital in 1960, hoping that this would spur the region's development. But the plan did not initially work out well. While Brasília grew, the rest of the region did not. In the 1970s, however, the central-west boomed. About 100,000 people moved in each year, making it Brazil's "Wild West." Landowners still hire *pistoleiros* ("piss-toh-LEH-rohs") to keep squatters off their property, and guns often replace the law in frontier towns.

Almost all of the region sits on the Central Plateau, a huge plain 3,300 feet (1,006 m) above sea level. Scrub brush and small trees cover most of the land, but rich, red soil lies underneath. The region has already become a major cattle-raising area, and increasing amounts of land are being cultivated. Many people fear that settlers pouring into the region will cause serious damage to the environment, and this may alter the ecology of the entire world. Farmers use the slash-and-burn technique to prepare new fields: they cut down the vegetation and then burn it. Satellites have detected heat from thousands of small fires in the region, and scientists fear that this is contributing to the warming of the planet.

Economic development also threatens the Grand Pantanal, a low swampland off the Central Plateau along the Paraguay River. Pollution from mining and the growth of cattle herds endanger the fragile balance of this wildlife preserve along the border with Bolivia and Paraguay.

Rains flood the Grand Pantanal between October and April. Over 350 types of fish thrive on the plants in the swollen rivers and spawn during this period. Then comes the dry season, when water levels fall, trapping fish in landlocked lakes. These fish make easy prey for the 600 species of birds that nest in the Grand Pantanal. Alligators also feed on these fish and are hunted for their skins, which fetch a good price on the international market.

Yet humans are not the ultimate predators in the Grand Pantanal. When piranhas get trapped in lakes in the dry season, their normal diet of small fish runs out, and they turn to larger animals and even people for food.

An alligator in the evergreen Grand Pantanal, a natural wildlife swampland covering 40,000 square miles (103,600 square km).

THE NORTHEAST

Nine states along the Atlantic coast make up the northeastern region, approximately 18 percent of Brazil's territory. This was the first area to be colonized by the Portuguese, and it is still a historical and cultural center. It is also the least developed part of the country, with little industry and poor agriculture.

Severe drought regularly plagues the northeastern region. The worst droughts came between 1877 and 1919, causing two million deaths. The most recent disaster, a five-year drought that ended in 1984, forced thousands to move to crowded cities or to the central-western frontier.

A narrow, fertile strip follows the coastline from the city of Natal south through the state of Bahia. Here, cocoa and sugarcane plantations thrive if there is enough rain. A line of white sandy beaches along the coast makes

this a popular area for tourists. The major coastal cities of Recife, Maceió, and Salvador all have beautiful beaches and areas of historical interest.

Beyond the majestic beaches lies the immense dry backland known as the *sertão* ("seh-TAUN"). Only cactus and scrub brush break up the dusty brown earth in this zone. Rain never falls during the first six months of the year; then it comes in sudden storms. A few hours will produce most of the rainfall for an entire year, and flash floods can be a problem. Life is very difficult for the inhabitants of this region who try to squeeze out a living by raising cattle.

One major river, the São Francisco, breaks up the dry scenery of the *sertão*. It serves as a source of water and energy and as a means of transportation for the region. Barges and ferries patrol the 1,800-mile (2,897-km) river, including a U.S. steamboat built in 1913 for use on the Mississippi River. The river's water enables some farming to take place along its banks. The Paulo Afonso dam and power plant in Bahia also generate electricity for much of the region.

Cars ready for export at the port in Rio de Janeiro. Manufactured products make up about 70 percent of Brazil's exports.

THE SOUTHEAST

The southeast is the most developed, industrialized, and populated region. Made up of the states of Minas Gerais, Espírito Santo, Rio de Janeiro, and São Paulo, the southeast accounts for only 11 percent of the nation's land, but contains the three largest cities—São Paulo, Rio de Janeiro, and Belo Horizonte—and 44 percent of the national population. The region's moderate climate makes it an important agricultural area and has also encouraged settlement and the growth of industry.

São Paulo is the business capital of Brazil, accounting for a third of the nation's industrial output. One of the largest cities in the world, São Paulo has a metropolitan population of 17.7 million people, many of whom come from other parts of the world. Millions of Brazilians have also poured into the city from the northeast.

Brazilians fondly call Rio de Janeiro, a city of 11.1 million residents, the *Cidade Maravilhosa*, or Marvelous City. The *Pão de Açúcar*, or Sugar Loaf, mountain, is a bare granite rock guarding the entrance to the Guanabara Bay. A string of beautiful beaches, starting with Copacabana and Ipanema, lines the coast. In spite of having lost its roles as the leading business center and the nation's capital, Rio remains Brazil's top tourist destination.

Belo Horizonte is the capital of Minas Gerais. Located on a high plateau about 2,500 feet (762 m) above sea level, Minas Gerais has been an important mining center for 300 years. Three-quarters of the world's gold found in the 18th century came from Minas Gerais. Today, it is a major source of iron ore and valuable gems.

Most of the state of São Paulo sits on this same plateau. Here, the red soil and temperate climate are perfect for growing coffee, and this has financed the growth of São Paulo. Today, Brazil is by far the world's top exporter of coffee.

Sugar Loaf Mountain, a well-known landmark, towers over Rio de Janeiro, the Marvellous City.

THE SOUTH

The smallest of the five regions, the south is a cattle and agricultural center. Its three states all fall below the Tropic of Capricorn. The temperate climate has attracted European immigrants from Italy and Germany.

A low mountain range dominates the region, starting in the center of the state of Rio Grande do Sul and ending at the Central Plateau. The south of Rio Grande do Sul is a flat grassland, an extension of the *pampas* of Argentina. This is still Brazil's main cattle-raising area. Residents here are called *gauchos*, after the cowboys who round up the herds on the *pampas*.

The Paraná River dominates Brazil's third major river system. It joins the Paraguay River in Argentina before emptying into the Atlantic Ocean. At the point where Brazil meets Argentina and Paraguay lies the Iguaçu Falls.

Gauchos—Brazil's cowboys—herding livestock around the *pampas* of the south.

A winter wonderland. The south is the only region in Brazil that receives snowfall and has four seasons.

Water pours over 275 waterfalls spread over two miles (3.2 km), producing a roar that can be heard several miles away. The most spectacular view is at Devil's Throat, where 14 falls curve around a 269-foot (82-m) drop.

Itaipú Dam, the heart of the world's largest hydroelectric plant, lies along the border with Paraguay, a few miles from Iguaçu Falls. It is a complex of five dams stretching three miles (4.8 km). At its highest point, one dam soars more than a mile (1.6 km) above ground level. The dam's reservoir is also Brazil's largest lake. Brazil and Paraguay combined efforts in 1975 to build this project, which began generating electricity in 1984 and was completed in the early 1990s.

CLIMATE

Temperatures and rainfall vary for different parts of the country. In the north, it is humid with heavy rainfall all year round. In the coastal areas, it is hot, with slightly less rainfall. In the central regions, it is semi-humid—hot and wet in the summer and drier and cooler in the winter. In the south, it is humid with regular rainfall and occasional snowfall and frost.

HISTORY

THE EARLIEST INHABITANTS of Brazil were the Indians. However, the country's recorded history begins with the arrival of the Portuguese. In 1500, eight years after Christopher Columbus arrived in America, Sailor Pedro Álvares Cabral arrived in Brazil.

Cabral had set off from Portugal for India via the coast of Africa. Many previously thought that he found South America by accident, after winds blew him off course. However, modern historians believe that the Portuguese had already suspected land lay to the west of Africa and sent Cabral to find it.

At that time, Spain and Portugal, being Europe's main imperial powers, were sending explorers to the Americas, Africa, and India. In 1494, the two countries signed the Treaty of Tordesillas, an agreement that would divide newly discovered lands between them. They drew a line from north to south down the world map and agreed that all lands found to the east of the line would belong to Portugal, while all lands found to the west would go to Spain.

When Cabral landed in northeastern Brazil, he stood to the east of the line, giving Portugal a legal claim to part of Spanish America. He sailed to India only two weeks later. Portugal did little to develop its new property, except to send an occasional fleet to collect some *pau brazil* ("pow brah-SEEL"), a wood from which the Europeans extracted red dye. It was this wood that gave the new colony its name.

Above: **Portuguese colonists erect a cross, while their comrades try to communicate with the indigenous Indians.**

Opposite: **A church in the historic town of Ouro Prêto, or Black Gold. In the 18th century, Ouro Prêto was the center of a gold rush. Today the town has the country's purest Baroque art collection and architecture.**

THE INDIANS

According to findings in the state of Piauí, Brazil was already inhabited by groups of hunter-gatherers as early as 47,000 years ago. Most experts believe that these hunters made their way from Asia to Brazil via North America. The experts estimate that about four million indigenous Indians were living in Brazil when Pedro Álvares Cabral arrived in 1500.

Colonizers from Europe did not bring prosperity and progress to the Indians. Instead, the Portuguese unwittingly infected and killed thousands of Indians with new diseases such as measles and smallpox. The Portuguese also tried to force the Indians to work on their sugar plantations. Unable to resist the colonizers, many Indians fled to the interior. Those who remained on the coast assimilated into society by marrying the Portuguese colonists and African slaves. Today, only about 220,000 Indians survive; almost all live in the Amazonian region.

EXPANSION IN THE COLONIAL PERIOD

The Portuguese king paid little attention to Brazil until he realized other Europeans would take over the colony if he did not act. He handed out land titles, and in 1534 settlers founded the cities of Olinda and Vitória. The king established a colonial government in the new city of Salvador da Bahia in 1549. In 1567, the Portuguese founded the city of Rio de Janeiro on a site from which they had just expelled a group of French settlers.

In 1580, politics again boosted Brazil's development. Portugal became part of Spain, making Brazil a target for Spain's enemies—Holland and France. The Dutch invaded and conquered parts of the northeastern coast between 1630 and 1654, while the French briefly seized what is now the state of Maranhão. The challenge of expelling the invaders brought more people to the colony. In 1625, 70 ships carrying more than 12,000 men sailed from Portugal to help the inhabitants fight the Dutch.

The growing number of settlers spurred the exploration of Brazil's interior. Frontiersmen called *bandeirantes* ("bahn-day-RAHN-tehs"), or flag bearers, led marches as far south as Argentina, as far west as Bolivia, and as far north as the Amazon River. The *bandeirantes* established Brazil's claim to lands far west of the Treaty of Tordesillas.

Orange Fortress on Itamaraca Island is a reminder of Brazil's colonial history.

THE BANDEIRANTES

When the *bandeirantes* set off from São Vincente (modern-day São Paulo) at the end of the 16th century, their main purpose was to capture Indians to sell as slaves to plantation owners. The Indians of the northeast fled inland to escape the *bandeirantes*. Ironically, the *bandeirantes* depended on the Indians to guide them on their trips. Some groups of Indians helped the hunters capture rival groups.

Antonio Raposo Tavares was one of the most notorious *bandeirantes*. In 1648, he set off from São Vincente with 200 colonists and 1,000 Indians. He destroyed several Jesuit missions along the Paraguayan border, sending the Indians who lived there off to slavery. He then proceeded north along the Paraguay River, until he reached territories that now lie in Bolivia. From there, he followed the Madeira River and then the Amazon, until he reached the Atlantic. In 1651, after traveling more than 3,000 miles (4,828 km), he returned with only 59 men.

After Brazil began transporting African slaves to work on the plantations, the *bandeirantes* began prospecting for gold. They found it in Minas Gerais in 1693, setting off a gold rush that drew thousands of settlers to Brazil's center.

The monument to the *bandeirantes* in São Paulo. The *bandeirantes* were considered the all-purpose frontiersmen, who usually had European fathers and Indian mothers. From his Indian heritage, the *bandeirante* had superb scouting and survival skills; from his European side, his desire for wealth and adventure sent him roaming the entire country.

SLAVERY IN BRAZIL

Slaves from Africa played just as big a part in Brazil's development as Portuguese colonists did. Slaves began arriving as early as 1516. At the time of independence in 1822, an estimated two million slaves made up over half the population. Their numbers reached about 3.6 million before the slave trade was abolished. The slaves did not submit willingly to their fate. Many escaped from their masters to the unsettled hills of the interior, where they formed independent colonies called *quilombos* ("kee-LOHM-boos"). The most famous, Quilombo dos Palmares, had a population of 30,000. It survived for 76 years before it was crushed in 1694.

After Brazil gained independence, a movement to end slavery slowly grew. The emperor's daughter, Princess Isabel, took the final steps in implementing it. In 1871, while her father was away, she convinced the Brazilian Congress to grant freedom at birth to the children of slaves. Then in 1888, the last slaves were finally given their freedom. Brazil was the last country in the Western Hemisphere to abolish slavery.

INDEPENDENCE AND EMPIRE

Events in Europe set the stage for Brazil's independence. In 1807, Napoleon's army conquered Portugal. King João fled to Rio de Janeiro, making Brazil the only colony ever to become the seat of power for an empire. Before returning to Portugal 14 years later, King João established an effective system of government and left his son, Dom Pedro, to rule Brazil. When King João returned to Portugal, he found a hostile parliament insisting that Brazil be ruled from Lisbon. It demanded the return of Dom Pedro. Judging that the Brazilians would fight for independence rather than return to colonial status, Dom Pedro decided to stay. On September 7, 1822, he proclaimed Brazil's independence. Three months later, he was crowned the "constitutional emperor and perpetual defender" of Latin America's only empire.

The perpetual defender lasted only nine years. Brazilians wanted more popular participation in government, but Dom Pedro ruled as an absolute monarch. He fought constantly with the new Brazilian Congress and lost popular support when Brazil lost southern territories in a war against Argentina. In 1831, Dom Pedro abdicated and returned to Portugal. He left behind as heir his 6-year-old son, Dom Pedro II.

REIGN OF DOM PEDRO II

Following Dom Pedro's departure, rebellion broke out in the northeast and south, and the country appeared to be on the brink of disintegration. In 1840, the congress turned in desperation to Dom Pedro II and made the 15-year-old ruler of Brazil.

Incredibly, Dom Pedro II proved equal to the task. His 49-year rule marked the most stable and progressive stretch in Brazil's history. He granted more power to the congress, but used his authority and personal prestige to keep the upper hand in government.

The emperor encouraged agricultural growth and immigration. As a result, by 1888, over 100,000 Europeans were immigrating annually to southeastern Brazil. Most of them went to work on coffee plantations in São Paulo, since coffee production by that time was responsible for over half of the country's exports.

Dom Pedro II also promoted education, health, and welfare. His most important achievement was the abolition of slavery in 1888. Dom Pedro II firmly established Brazil's southern borders through battles with neighboring countries. The hardest struggle started in 1865. It took five years for Brazil, allied with Uruguay and Argentina, to defeat Paraguay in this war.

These military campaigns increased the size and stature of the Brazilian army. Military officers became more powerful and began to involve themselves in politics, a development that eventually led to the emperor's downfall. In the 20th century, the military would become Brazil's most powerful political institution.

Emperor Dom Pedro II. This extraordinary but humble man brought much-needed peace to Brazil, giving it the longest period of political stability. He did not adopt the autocratic ways of his father but guided the nation with personal authority. Sadly, Brazil's most popular leader was forced into exile in 1889 when the military overthrew his government.

THE REPUBLIC

Getúlio Vargas represented a total break from Brazil's previous rural-controlled politics. Instead, Brazilian politics began to be dominated by people from the fast-growing urban areas.

The prosperous era of Dom Pedro II ended in November 1889. Having lost the support of the landowners through the abolition of slavery, he could not resist a revolt led by the military. He went into exile, and the military proclaimed a new republic of the United States of Brazil. Forty disorderly years followed. The republic had a president and congress as well as regular elections. But conflicting regional interests made their jobs difficult, and the military continued to play an active role in politics. Between 1889 and 1930, 13 presidents held office.

In 1930, a military coup placed a civilian from the state of Rio Grande do Sul, Getúlio Vargas, in power. He represented a new kind of leader: a populist who depended on the support of the urban masses instead of the rich landowners. Vargas legalized labor unions, passed a minimum wage law, and instituted a social security system. He also made himself a dictator, first by rewriting the constitution, then by canceling elections. In 1945, the military ousted him and restored democracy. He was reelected president in 1951 and was succeeded in 1954 by Juscelino Kubitschek.

MILITARY RULE

In the 1950s, vast sums of money were spent on building Brasília, hydroelectric plants, highways, and other economic projects. This set the stage for future growth, but also brought immediate economic problems by plunging the nation into debt. Another coup followed, but this time the military retained power. From 1964 to 1985, Brazil was ruled by a succession of five army generals. The 1970s were the decade of the Brazilian Miracle, when industry grew at a spectacular rate and provided thousands of jobs. But political freedom disappeared, and thousands of people were forced into exile or arrested on political grounds.

BRAZIL IN WORLD WAR II

When Brazil declared war on Germany in 1942, it became the first South American country to enter the conflict. The 25,000-strong Brazilian Expeditionary Force that went to Italy in 1944 was the first South American army to engage in battle overseas. The force served until the end of the war under the command of the U.S. Fifth Army.

Another contribution was the airfield in Natal, in the northeast. Most aircraft at that time could not fly nonstop across the Atlantic. In 1942, U.S. planes stopped at Natal on their way to providing supplies to Allied troops in North Africa, the Middle East, and even China. Brazil had entered the war because it felt that with its size and resources, it needed to play a role in world affairs. The country made worthy and immensely vital contributions to the ending of the war.

The economy stopped growing in the 1980s, and Brazil again was unable to pay back its loans. Frustrated by the debt and by growing public discontent, the military handed power back to a civilian government in 1985. In 1998, Fernando Henrique Cardoso was reelected after his first victory in 1995.

GOVERNMENT

BRAZIL IS A FEDERAL REPUBLIC under the leadership of a president whose powers are similar to those of the president of the United States.

THE NEW REPUBLIC

During Brazil's 20 years of military rule, the army had almost complete control of the government, and the congress wielded little power. Since 1985, however, the government of Brazil has been in the hands of civilians; Brazil is said to have entered the era of the "New Republic."

In the New Republic, political power lies in the hands of the president and congress. The president needs congressional approval for many acts, but like the president of the United States, he or she can veto laws passed by the congress. The president also plays an important role in state politics and has the power to intervene in state affairs, calling in federal troops if necessary. As the states cannot levy taxes on their own, they depend on the president to finance their budgets.

The president is supported by a vice-president and a cabinet consisting of state ministers. In September 1992, President Itamar Franco formed an administration that included representatives of all the main parties. Franco inherited the presidency when his predecessor, Fernando Collor de Mello, was impeached by the congress for corruption and drug abuse, high inflation rates, and economic recession.

Since independence in 1822, Brazil's constitution has been rewritten seven times. The constitution of October 1988 contained a clause requiring a poll to be conducted in 1993 to decide whether to switch from a presidential system of government to a parliamentary system.

In April 1993, a referendum was held to decide the issue. The result was in favor of retaining the presidential system of government, with almost 70 percent of all votes cast.

Opposite: **The government buildings of Brasília cast their reflection in a pool. The capital of Brazil was the brainchild of Juscelino Kubitschek, who served as president in the 1950s. The project showed the dynamism of Kubitschek's administration, but it also drained the country of much of its money, leaving huge debts and high inflation.**

THE BASICS OF GOVERNMENT

Brazil is a federal republic made up of 26 states and the Federal District of Brasília. The government is divided into the executive, legislative, and judicial branches. The president and cabinet make up the executive branch. The president serves a five-year term and cannot be reelected.

The legislature consists of a congress divided into two bodies: a senate and a chamber of deputies. The senate has 81 members, three elected from each state, while the chamber has 513 deputies, at least three from each state. Senators serve eight-year terms, while deputies hold office for four years. Both can run for reelection. Each state has a democratically elected governor and legislature. States are divided into counties called *municipios* ("moo-nee-SEE-pee-ohs"), each of which has an elected mayor and a local council.

In the judiciary, an 11-member Supreme Court has the final say in all legal matters. Federal and state courts fall below the Supreme Court. Special federal courts handle cases involving labor, military, juvenile, and election issues.

The 1988 constitution protects several rights for citizens: freedom of speech, freedom of the press, freedom to assemble peacefully, and freedom for workers to go on strike. It also permits citizens to require the government to release all information it has gathered on them. The latest change in the constitution gave Indians full rights as citizens for the first time and guaranteed Indian groups the rights to all resources falling within their land.

ARMY COLONELS

Two types of colonels complicate the operation of Brazil's democracy. The first are officers of the military. In the last 100 years, they have become Brazil's strongest political institution. All officers are taught that it is their duty to ensure the nation's security; in the past, they have intervened in instances they considered a threat to law and order.

Since the 1940s, the military has stood watch against any movement connected in the slightest way with Communism. The military took over the government in 1964, because it believed the president planned to make himself a Communist dictator.

After 21 years in power, the military gave up the presidency to a civilian, publicly guaranteeing that they would not get involved in politics again. But Brazilians know that the threat of intervention still exists.

The power of the military is undeniable in Brazilian politics. The armed forces ruled Brazil from 1964 to the mid-1980s.

HONORARY COLONELS

The second type of colonel has nothing to do with the military. The title of honorary colonel derives from the state government's dependence on the National Guard in 1850 to maintain law and order in Brazil's northeast. The wealthy landowners competed for the prestige of being named the colonel in charge.

These colonels became the most important political leaders in their counties. They were the chief law enforcers and supervisors of general elections. They also served as the government's main source of local news as well as its main supporter in the region. They became the middlemen between the government, which depended on them to deliver election votes, and the voters, who depended on them to get what they needed from the government.

As time passed, the National Guard lost its importance and the colonels disappeared. But honorary colonels remain. The wealthiest and most influential men are called colonels.

These men are still the main link between the capital and the countryside. They marshal votes for the governor, who repays their district with special favors. In a land of little education and low pay, citizens vote for the colonel's candidates, because they believe if they help the colonel, he may return the favor.

POLITICAL AWARENESS

The colonels have dominated Brazilian politics for 150 years. But there are signs that their importance is fading.

Most Brazilians now live in cities, so the rural vote has lost some of its importance. The colonels also associated themselves with the military

Brazilians tell of one town in the state of Pernambuco that has been run by the same family since 1848. At the start of the 1980s, the mayor was the cousin of the district judge, who was the cousin of the civil registrar, who was the cousin of the former public prosecutor, who was the cousin of the district's congressman.

government, and then lost prestige along with the army generals when they gave up power. Finally, the growth of the media has made it harder for the colonels to manipulate voters.

Before the spread of radio and television, Brazilians living outside the cities only knew the local news. Since the colonels dominated the news, people usually saw fit to vote as the colonels wished. Now they are more aware of national issues and of people who are more powerful.

Previously, election candidates could only reach voters through the colonels. Now they can speak directly to all via radio and television. This has led to the growth of national political parties, the largest being the Brazilian Democratic Movement (PMDB).

Brazilians young and old celebrate at a political rally in Rio de Janeiro.

All Brazilians between the ages of 18 and 70 are obliged to vote. Even teenagers aged 16 and 17 can vote if they wish. Voting is also voluntary for senior citizens over 70 years, illiterate people, and prisoners in jail.

PATRONAGE

In modern Brazil, politics still revolves around people, not parties. In the 1989 elections, the PMDB candidate finished far behind Collor de Mello, who overcame the weakness of his party with his charismatic personality and was able to impress voters and form alliances with local leaders.

In the eyes of voters, having friends in the right places is generally more useful than having good ideas. Leaders with good ideas are not good candidates if they cannot get anything done. And to get things done, they have to know people and be able to make deals.

ECONOMY

THE BRAZILIAN ECONOMY boomed in the 1970s. The people believed their country was destined to be a major world power. The sleeping giant, they said, had finally awoken. During the years of the "Brazilian Miracle," the government spent billions of dollars on large-scale projects such as the Trans-Amazon Highway, underground subways for Rio de Janeiro and São Paulo, and a nuclear power plant. Most of these were financed by loans from foreign banks. As a result of these projects, Brazil experienced spectacular growth. Between 1968 and 1973, economic growth averaged 10 percent per year.

However, when recession hit in the early 1980s and inflation soared, Brazil's economy ran into trouble. Although the situation has now improved, one of the greatest problems facing Brazil is how to pay off its foreign debt of $120 billion.

Above: **A link across the heart of the Amazon. The Trans-Amazon Highway cuts through the jungle as far as the eye can see.**

Opposite: **A fish market in Belém, Brazil.**

INFLATION

Throughout the 1980s, Brazil suffered high inflation rates that almost crippled the economy. In 1990, when annual inflation reached 4,854 percent, the government was forced to rename the currency and reduce its value by 1,000. So 1,000 new *cruzados*, as the former currency was called, became one *cruzeiro*.

Although the government adjusted wages based on inflation, wages and savings still could not keep up. As a result, people looked for other ways to avoid losing money. Many converted their cash to U.S. dollars, sometimes at more than twice the official exchange rate.

A child peddles products in the city. Thousands of homeless children have to fend for themselves because their parents cannot support them.

ECONOMIC PROBLEMS

Despite tremendous progress in the last 30 years, life for many Brazilians has not improved. The majority of people do not share in the nation's wealth. Over half of the workers earn less than $200 a month. Together, they earn less than the richest 1 percent of society.

In the northeast, people have a life expectancy of 55, while for those in the southeast, it is 67. Eight out of 10 children in northeastern Brazil suffer from malnutrition.

Every major city has its share of slums, called *favelas* ("fah-VEY-lahs"), on the fringes. About two-fifths of the residents of Rio de Janeiro live in *favelas.* By the age of 13, most slum children are on the streets shining shoes, selling gum, begging, or stealing. Children in *favelas* have little chance of acquiring an education or a well-paid job. Changing this pattern is the biggest challenge facing Brazil today.

ECONOMIC GIANT

As the eighth largest economy in the world, Brazil is also: the largest exporter of coffee and orange juice; the second largest producer of soybeans, sugarcane, cocoa, tin, and iron ore; the third largest producer of corn and bauxite; the fifth largest producer of gold and exporter of military weapons; the seventh largest producer of steel; and the eighth largest car manufacturer.

Brazil is also a world leader in one very undesirable category: it owes foreign banks $120 billion, the largest debt of any developing country. This means every man, woman, and child living in Brazil owes foreign banks more than $780,000.

MINERAL WEALTH

Brazil has enormous mineral wealth. Besides having one-third of the world's iron ore reserves, it also has the largest bauxite reserves in Latin America. Other mineral deposits include manganese, aluminum, tin, zinc, and coal. However, it is gold that draws thousands to the mines.

Brazil's most famous gold discovery came in January 1980 at Serra Pelada. Since then, independent miners called *garimpeiros* ("gahr-im-PAY-rohs") have been struggling through piles of mud, like ants streaming around an anthill, carrying about 25 tons (25,000 kg) of dirt out of the mine each year.

Gold prospectors have also become rich in the Rondônia and Roraima rivers. Major deposits in Roraima, along the Venezuelan border, have caused problems as they are located near the Yanomami Indian reservation. The government has prohibited *garimpeiros* from working there, but so far, the lure of gold has outweighed such laws.

Besides invading Indian land, the *garimpeiros* cause other problems. They use mercury to separate gold from the soil, thereby polluting the rivers. Working conditions are unhealthy, and the *garimpeiros* suffer from tropical diseases. They also have to look out for tricky businessmen looking to con them out of their gold.

Still, the mining continues. In the hills of Pará and along the riverbanks of the Roraima and Rondônia, hope lives. *Garimpeiros* believe that anyone can become rich with the right combination of hard work and luck.

The gold camp of Serra Pelada. Officials estimate about two-thirds of the gold mined here is smuggled out of the country.

Harvesting sugarcane.

When the government offered settlers in Rondônia 247-acre (about 1-square km) plots of land, it quickly had a waiting list of 20,000 families and had to stop accepting new applications. Wealthy land-owners established huge farms and ranches.

FARMLAND

One of the world's largest agricultural states, Brazil produces coffee, soybeans, sugarcane, cocoa beans, tobacco, cotton, corn, rice, fruit, and potatoes. The country's agricultural sector contributes about 40 percent of export revenues. Cattle raising is a major farming activity in the northeast and south. Brazil is the world's fourth largest cattle-producing country.

Land ownership is a big issue in Brazil. About 20 percent of all Brazilians live in the countryside, but few till their own land. About 5 percent of the population own 80 percent of the land.

The government has tried to redistribute land wealth by implementing a law that allows it to buy unused private property to give to those who do not own land. However, this law has not been received well on either side of the dispute. Landowners feel the government's payment falls far below the value of their property, while peasants feel the government is too slow in enforcing this law. Some peasants have tried occupying unused property illegally, and landowners have responded by hiring gunmen to keep intruders out. The decades-long conflict over land ownership in Brazil has resulted in the loss of thousands of lives.

An assembly line of AMX jets in São Paulo. Brazil is one of the world's largest manufacturers of military weapons.

INDUSTRY

While the government has tried to encourage people to move to the country's interior, its main objective for the last three decades has been to promote the country's industry.

The government has borrowed billions of dollars to finance projects supporting industrial growth and expansion. It has invited foreign companies to establish plants and imposed high tariffs on imported goods to discourage local consumption of foreign products. The government has also established state-run companies to control key industries such as oil, steel, communications, and electricity.

Brazil's industries have grown considerably in the past 25 years. Its automotive industry is the eighth largest in the world. Other sectors that have contributed to employment and industrial development are: food and beverages, tobacco, petrochemicals, clothing manufacturing, footwear, cement, and electrical and electronic industries.

Industrial development has boosted Brazil's exports. In July 2001, Brazil had a trade surplus of US$108 million. While imports amounted to US$4.8 billion, exports totaled US$4.9 billion.

ENVIRONMENT

BRAZIL IS UNMATCHED in South America in natural wealth and beauty. The world's fifth largest country, Brazil is home to the largest rain forest and the deepest and second longest river in the world, both named Amazon after Greek legend. Brazil is one of the most biologically diverse countries in the world and the most diverse in South America. For all of this, Brazil is also a land where environmental concerns come face to face with human need and sometimes greed.

NATURE'S RICHES PILED HIGH

Since Brazil is a large and ecologically varied country, it is perhaps not surprising that it ranks as one of the world's most biologically diverse areas in the sheer number of plant and animal species found here. The country has the largest number of species of primates—the order that includes humans—and also ranks first in the number of plant and amphibian species.

Brazil ranks third in the world in the number of bird species and fourth in the number of butterfly and reptilian species. Brazilian flora and fauna live in a variety of environments, including dry forests, rain forests, mountain and lowland forests, marshes, semiarid scrub lands, and savannah.

Below: **The macaw lives in the Amazon rain forest.**

Opposite: **Giant water lilies at Rio Badajos in the Amazon river basin.**

As well as having many different ecosystems and a wide variety of plants and animals, Brazil also has a high degree of endemism. This means that many species of flora and fauna living in the country are found nowhere else on the planet. The implication of so many unique species is that environmental protection here is far more important than in countries that host more common plants and animals.

Brazil hosted the United Nations Conference on the Environment and Development—more commonly known as the Earth Day Summit—in Rio de Janeiro in 1992 and negotiated agreements on sustainable development. However, there have been laws protecting wildlife, forests, and waterways in the country since the 1930s, long before the summit put Brazil on the environmental map.

The most recent constitution provides for environmental protection measures that are advanced in comparison to many other countries. There are several government bodies looking out for the environment, such as a permanent Commission for the Defense of the Consumer, the Environment, and Minorities, as well as a Brazilian Institute for the Environment and Renewable Natural Resources. There is also a ministry devoted to the environment, hydraulic resources (water), and the Amazon.

In addition to these government bodies, there are a number of non-governmental organizations working to protect the environment, including the SOS Atlantic Rain Forest Foundation, working to preserve the Atlantic rain forest ecosystem, and the Amazon Working Group, dedicated to the Amazon river basin and forest.

Brazilians are aware of the natural treasures within their national borders. There are laws protecting indigenous forests and wildlife, and there are people dedicated to putting these laws to use.

IGUAÇU NATIONAL PARK

Located in southwestern Paraná, Iguaçu covers 42,000 acres (170 square km) of protected area. Most of the park is subtropical rain forest, where plants such as tree ferns, liana vines, and epiphytes flourish. Epiphytes are plants that can grow without roots. The seeds attach themselves to the branches of trees, and the growing plant absorbs moisture and nutrients directly from the air, without harming the host tree. Animals that make Iguaçu their home include the ocelot, jaguar, puma, giant otter, American tapir, bush dog, giant anteater, broad-nosed caiman, and a variety of birds such as the Harpy eagle. Both the glaucus macaw and black-fronted piping guan are local birds on the endangered list.

The Iguaçu National Park was named a World Heritage Site in 1986, partly because it contains the Brazilian share of the Iguaçu Falls (*below*). This fantastic waterfall is one of the world's largest and extends over a two-mile (3.2-km) area. The water drops 269 feet (82 m) down a giant stairway, and the mist created keeps the surrounding land and the islands in the river covered in lush vegetation. Although the park is a protected site, it is threatened by poachers and people who raid the forests looking for palm trees that produce palm hearts used in salads.

The Iguaçu falls were featured in the 1986 movie *The Mission*, starring Robert De Niro, Jeremy Irons, Aidan Quinn, and Liam Neeson. The movie is about the Jesuits who tried to protect Guaraní Indians from Brazilian slave raiders in the 1700s.

PROBLEMS

Despite its great size and potential, Brazil faces many serious environmental challenges and threats. The most famous of these is the destruction of the Amazon rain forest, the earth's lungs. In the 1970s and 1980s, this forest was cleared at a rate of about 13,670 square miles (22,000 square km) a year, resulting in an accumulated loss of about 15 percent of the forest.

Contrary to popular belief, most of the deforestation then was done by large commercial interests rather than by impoverished peasants. The government at the time encouraged economic growth through expansion of land under agricultural production, and that meant that large swathes of forest were made available to those who were willing to burn it down and make pasture for cattle. Deforestation continued even in later years, when economic crises and slowdowns reduced the rate of forest clearing and public opinion against this strategy began to grow. In 1995, a single burning season destroyed 11,197 square miles (29,000 square km) of the Amazon—the size of New Jersey and Connecticut. About 4,246 square miles (11,000 square km) are still being cleared each year.

Other areas in Brazil, such as the dry northeast, are also under threat from human activities. Clearing land in the northeast for cattle has resulted in soil erosion and desertification. The Atlantic forests are nearly gone, and several plants and animals that are endemic or unique to this ecosystem now face extinction. Mining activities all over the country result in land degradation and water pollution. Gold mining in particular relies on the use of poisonous substances like mercury and cyanide to separate the gold from silt. Damaging the environment is not restricted to rural areas. Cities generate huge amounts of air and water pollution, due to overcrowding and inadequate facilities.

SAVING THE RAIN FOREST: WHAT'S ALL THE FUSS ABOUT?

Many people are aware of the urgent need to protect the world's forests, especially the Amazon. However, few understand exactly why these forests are so important, except that they are home to beautiful animals and plants. There are many reasons to protect the forests, but perhaps one of the most important is that they are the lungs of the planet.

As the Sun warms the earth, the earth radiates some of the Sun's heat back into space. Greenhouse gases, such as carbon dioxide, methane, nitrous oxide, and ozone, retain heat in the earth's atmosphere. (Nitrogen and oxygen, which make up most of our "air," do not retain heat.) The planet needs small amounts of these greenhouse gases to provide a hospitable environment for life.

Before people began using fossil fuels and burning up forests, the forests were a key part of the equation in maintaining a balance between heat-retaining and other gases. Volcanic activity produced most of the carbon dioxide, which forests absorbed and converted into oxygen and cellulose.

Today, we face two related problems: about half the forests are gone; and industrial activity has released billions of tons of additional carbon dioxide into the atmosphere. This means that more heat is retained in the atmosphere, leading to global warming. Scientists predict that there will be at least a 1.8ºF (1ºC) overall warming of the atmosphere by 2030 and a 5.4ºF (3ºC) increase before 2100. This could have disastrous results, including the melting of polar ice caps and flooding of coastlines (where about 50 percent of all people live). Drastic changes in weather patterns will alter environments, leading to widespread extinction of plants and animals.

The two major sources of carbon dioxide are the burning of forests and the use of fossil fuels, which produce about 23 and 77 percent respectively of all carbon dioxide emissions. Brazil is the biggest culprit for forest burning, but the United States is the world's largest contributor of greenhouse gases, producing 22 percent of all greenhouse gas emissions. To help the planet "breathe" and keep our environment healthy for life, the Amazon has to be preserved and greenhouse gas emissions reduced.

Indigenous Indians demonstrate against the destruction of the Amazon rain forest.

SOLUTIONS

There are Brazilian organizations, such as the Landless Workers Movement, that are working to find a way to save the Amazon from human rampage. However, their success depends on cooperation from the rest of the world. Wealthy countries, especially, have to be committed to helping Brazil find more environmentally sound methods of creating energy and maintaining jobs and lifestyles. "People who live in glass houses shouldn't throw stones," as the saying goes. As long as countries with financial resources do not assume some of the responsibility of preserving the environment, it will be difficult for poorer countries to make adjustments necessary for the welfare of the global environment.

LAND USE: AN ENVIRONMENTALLY SOUND ANSWER

Brazil is a country with vast resources, both natural and human. Unfortunately, its history has created a situation in which very few people own most of the farmland even if they often do not cultivate it. In the meantime, the government has tried to resettle millions of landless rural workers onto newly cleared plots in the rain forest. This means that more forested land is being lost. Furthermore, since tropical soils are poor for agriculture, most small farmers end up abandoning their plots of land after a few years of trying to cultivate it.

The Landless Workers Movement has been working on another solution. They have organized thousands of rural families to occupy unused farmland, make it productive, and then claim legal ownership of the land in the courts. Since 1985, when the Catholic Church began to help organize poor rural people, the Landless Workers Movement has helped 250,000 families occupy and gain title to 15 million acres (60702.8 square km) of farmland. The movement has won international awards for its environmentally sound projects and for education. Once families form a new community on occupied land, they start a school, and the movement helps them find teachers for the children and tutors for the illiterate adults.

Although landowners who are unhappy with the movement have hired mercenaries to kill potential settlers and over a thousand people have lost their lives, most Brazilians support the movement. As powerful as the landowners may be, they may not be able to stop this movement of people determined to work and live from their nation's bounty.

BRAZILIANS

APART FROM ISOLATED GROUPS of indigenous Indians in the Amazon and recent immigrants from Europe and Asia, most Brazilians are either Caucasian or of mixed ethnicity. Africans, Indians, and Europeans have coexisted for 400 years, creating a mosaic of ethnic blends.

Children of African and European parents are called mulattos. *Caboclo* ("kah-BOH-cloh") children have European and Indian blood, and children of African and Indian parents are called *cafuso* ("kah-FOO-soh"). About 60 percent of Brazilians are Caucasian, 21 percent of mixed ethnicity, and 15 percent African. The remaining 4 percent include Indians, Asians, and other minorities.

Above: **Decades of experience show on the faces of these Brazilian women.**

Opposite: **A little girl from a Belém suburb shows why her village is called the "Village of Smiles."**

Despite being an ethnic melting pot, Brazil is still marked by strong regional differences. In general, the European influence is stronger in the south and southeast, while African culture dominates the states of Bahia and Rio de Janeiro as well as much of the northeast. Indian traditions have left their mark in the *sertão* in the northeast and in the northern and central-western regions.

More and more Brazilians are leaving the countryside to live in the crowded cities on the coast, especially São Paulo. As a result, *favelas,* or slums, sheltering thousands of poor immigrants in unhygienic conditions, have grown in almost every large city. About 40 percent of Rio de Janeiro's residents—over 5 million people—live in *favelas.*

47

POPULATION DISTRIBUTION

Brazil's growth rate has slowed in the last decade to 1.3 percent, down from more than 2 percent in the 1980s. Nevertheless, its population is still growing rapidly, and about two-thirds of Brazilians are below 30 years of age. Brazil has space for a large population if it is spread out, but most people choose or are forced to live in the cities, due to the lack of land and jobs in the countryside. Some 78 percent of Brazilians live in urban rather than rural areas, and a full 20 percent live in one of three cities: São Paulo, Rio de Janeiro, and Belo Horizonte. This creates pressure on cities to find space and provide services for the mushrooming populations.

BENÉ: "I WAS BORN A BLACK WOMAN"

Benedita da Silva is an Afro-Brazilian woman who has struggled all her life to make a difference. She was born in 1943 to poor plantation workers. Her parents, like many others, decided to try their luck in the big city and moved to Rio de Janeiro, where Bené grew up selling fruit and nuts in the streets to help her parents make ends meet. She and her 13 brothers and sisters knew poverty and hunger first hand. Bené had a fighting spirit. At 40, she returned to school to get a diploma and a university degree in social work. She was elected to Rio's city council in 1982. In 1986, she became the first black woman to sit in the Brazilian Congress. In 1994, Bené made history when she was elected to the senate. She was the first black woman to hold this prestigious position.

Throughout her career, Bené has tried to help Brazil's poor, the majority of whom are black. Afro-Brazilians have a shorter life expectancy, due to the harsh conditions of poverty, and a higher illiteracy rate (37 percent) than Caucasian Brazilians (15 percent). Ninety percent of Afro-Brazilian women have only elementary school education and earn only 48 percent of what Caucasian women earn for the same job. Although there is no legal discrimination in Brazil, being black often means being poor. People like Bené are working hard to change this. She was honored by one of Rio's samba schools in 1998.

A mother and her two children in a shantytown in Salvador. Though they make up 15 percent of the population, people of African ancestry often suffer discrimination in Brazil. They are still barred from some hotels and restaurants or told to enter through the back door. Brazil's leading civil rights advocates and churches are fighting to remove such barriers.

DISCRIMINATION

Brazil's constitution prohibits racial discrimination, and Brazilians are glad to not have to suffer racial strife in their country. Nonetheless, inequality among ethnic groups is a daily reality.

For example, dark-skinned men or women are rarely found in the congress or among army generals, corporate presidents, or diplomats. The average income and education level of Afro-Brazilians fall far below those of lighter-skinned Brazilians.

Many argue that this is not the product of racial discrimination. They argue instead that it is a reflection of the lack of opportunities for Afro-Brazilians, most of whom come from the poorer northeast. Whether it is racism or not, most Brazilians associate dark skin with the lower classes and discriminate against dark-skinned citizens.

Nevertheless, Brazilians frequently intermarry, and the number of intermarriages is on the rise. It is believed that over the past 40 years, the number of mulattos has greatly increased, while the percentage of whites and blacks in the population has dropped.

Young Indians hope to raise the consciousness of the nation to the plight of their people.

THE INDIANS

Today, almost all of Brazil's remaining 220,000 Indians live in the Amazon. The jungle still isolates them from the modern world, but civilization is breaking through. Brazilians face the challenge of integrating Indians into modern society without destroying Indian culture.

In 1961, the government's National Foundation for Assistance to Indians created the Xingu National Park to introduce modern tools and ideas to Indians. Some Indians have made the leap to modern society. In 1982, a leader of the Xingu group was elected to the national congress.

Open land and the promise of gold in Indian territories have attracted new settlers, who like the early European colonists, bring diseases and unfamiliar ideas with them. Some Indians are fighting to preserve their land and tradition. In 1991, backed by huge international support, the Yanomami won their claim for a reserve three times the size of Belgium. Many others still face the challenge of preserving their heritage while integrating into mainstream society.

SÃO PAULO: COSMOPOLITAN CENTER

More than any other city, São Paulo is a city of immigrants. For the past century, it has attracted the bulk of the country's European and Asian immigrants. From 1960 to 2000, a span of 40 years, São Paulo's population grew more than fourfold, from 3.8 million to 17.7 million.

Thousands of migrants, mostly from the northeast, live in the Bras neighborhood. Walking through Bras, you can hear the music of *violeiros* ("vee-oh-LAY-roos")—fiddlers who compose songs in response to challenges from their audience—and see street vendors peddling alligator skins and Amazonian herbs.

In the Bom Retiro neighborhood, Muslims, Jews, and Christians—descendants of immigrants from Lebanon, Syria, and Turkey—live peacefully in the thriving Middle Eastern shopping district.

A million São Paulo residents of Italian descent live in the Bela Vista neighborhood, a Little Italy with European-style *cantinas* ("cahn-TEE-nahs"). Every August, during a festival held in memory of the homeland, the residents consume 1,300 gallons (4,921 liters) of wine, three tons (3,000 kg) of spaghetti, and 40,000 pizzas.

Liberdade is home to most of São Paulo's 600,000 descendants of Japanese immigrants. Street signs in this neighborhood advertise in Japanese, and residents and visitors get to read three local Japanese newspapers, sign up for judo classes, and dine at authentic Asian restaurants.

Under two flags: this Japanese immigrant shows her support for Japan and Brazil. In 1908, the ship *Kasato Maru* arrived in Santos harbor with the first Japanese immigrants. They were seeking a new home, away from crop failures and earthquakes in Japan. Today, Japanese dominate São Paulo's Liberdade district.

AMERICANA

A unique group of immigrants founded the city of Americana, about an hour's drive from São Paulo. The city's seal tells its history: it features the stars and bars insignia of the Confederate States of America, flanked by two soldiers wearing the Confederate Army uniform.

After the end of the American Civil War in 1865, about three million Southerners from the defeated confederate states left America. A handful ended up in Brazil, where they started several settlements. Americana is the most prominent of the surviving settlements.

While most of its current 160,000 residents are descendants of later European immigrants, Americana's confederate heritage is obvious. Walking down the streets, you can still occasionally hear English spoken with a Southern accent. A monument in the downtown area honors confederate soldiers who died in the Civil War. Nearby stands a cemetery with the graves of confederate immigrants.

TYPICAL BRAZILIAN FIGURES

VAQUEIRO A *vaqueiro* ("vah-KAY-roo") is a cowboy who tends herds in the arid northeastern *sertão*. The *vaqueiro* are descendants of the African slaves and Portuguese settlers who left the coast and mixed with the Indians of the interior. They are stoic and struggle to survive in a hostile environment. Few amusements break up the monotony of their work, but annual round-ups and occasional rodeos offer them a chance to get together and show off their skills. Quiet, unemotional, and patient, they carry on with life. They are not so much fighters as they are survivors.

GAUCHO Life for the cowboys of the south is easier. The *gaucho* is a more colorful figure. Like his cousins in Argentina, Uruguay, and Paraguay, his forefathers hailed from Spain and married Indian women. At first they were outlaws who roamed the countryside, but they gained fame by helping in Argentina's fight for independence from Spain. Today, the *gaucho* is the symbol of machismo. Loud and abusive, he is used to getting his way. He brags about his three most prized possessions: his horse, knife, and wife. Known for his riding skills, he is also noted for the bitter *mate* ("MAH-cheh") tea that he brews and the *churrasco* ("shoo-HAHS-koo") meat that he barbecues.

A *baiana* in traditional dress.

SUYA This group is typical of the indigenous Indians of Brazil. They wear a disc in the lower lip, a distinguishing feature of some Amazonian groups. The Suya primarily fish and cultivate cassava plants. Because the soil in the Amazon is too thin to support extensive farming, the Suya generally live in small groups of about 60, with three or four families sharing all they grow or catch. Every two or three years, after exhausting the soil in one area, they move to a new patch of the forest.

BAIANO Perhaps the most powerful symbol of Brazil's African heritage, *baianos* ("bah-YAH-nohs") are residents of Bahia, the state with the largest population descended from slaves. In popular usage, the word *baiana* ("bah-YAH-nah") refers specifically to Afro-Brazilian women seen selling food on the city streets, wearing the traditional white clothing of their ancestors. They participate in special occasions like Salvador's Festival of Our Lord of Bonfim and Rio de Janeiro's Carnival.

53

LIFESTYLE

BRAZILIANS AMAZE OUTSIDERS with their ability to look on the bright side of life. Their optimism is even more remarkable in the face of their harsh reality.

A São Paulo television crew once interviewed a homeless family living under a highway. They were immigrants from the northeast, and they survived by rummaging through garbage cans for empty bottles or old newspapers to sell.

When the television crew asked the father how he was getting along, he said he was happy, adding "thanks be to God." The astonished interviewer asked what he had to be happy about. The father replied that his family could play cards together at night, or sing and dance together, and they had a transistor radio so they could listen to soccer match commentaries.

Most Brazilians believe that hard work and good intentions are not enough to change their lives. They believe that they are at the mercy of their environment, that authorities greater than the individual control society, and that spiritual powers determine the destiny of every human being. According to this rationale, no human effort can ever succeed without the support of a higher force, in particular, the support of the divine powers. It is no wonder then that Brazilians end most declarations with the phrase "if God wishes."

As a result of this view of life, Brazilians value the virtues of hierarchical organization, respecting authority and looking to those who hold high positions in society for guidance and leadership. Yet they remain cheerful in their belief that all forms of authority are flexible. The right balance of respect, intelligence, and patience can soften the will of anyone, from the local police captain to the president of the republic to God.

Above: **Yanomami Indians live in a communal hut in the middle of the Amazon rain forest.**

Opposite: **A Brazilian rides his donkey through town.**

AND GOD MADE BRAZILIANS ...

There is a joke that some Brazilians like to tell to laugh at their own shortcomings. It goes like this:

On the seventh day, as God was resting after having created the universe, the angel Gabriel came to compliment Him on His work. But the angel had one question. Was it fair for God to concentrate so much natural beauty, so much gold, so much rich soil, and so many lush forests and golden beaches in one country? Wasn't He being a bit partial toward Brazil?

"Don't worry, Gabriel," God answered, "things will even out. Wait till you see the lazy rascals I put to live there."

"WE'LL FIND A WAY"

In a society where rules are generally qute flexible, getting things done is a tricky, inexact science. *Jeito* ("JAY-toh"), meaning way, is the word used to describe this science. To Brazilians, the word evokes much more meaning. A person called a *jeitoso* ("jay-TOH-zoo") is a master at squirming out of difficult situations and solving complicated problems. When most people say some goal is impossible, a *jeitoso* promises to *dar um jeito* ("DAH oom JAY-toh"), or find a way. The key to *jeito* is knowing when and how to bend the rules. Sometimes the authority behind the rules is strong enough to force compliance. Other times, rules are just pointless obstacles that can, and should, be avoided.

Traffic laws offer a good example of this attitude. For Brazilian drivers in cities like Rio de Janeiro, a red traffic light does not always mean "stop." It means "stop" only if there is likely to be traffic. Late at night, when the streets are deserted, drivers see no reason to stop and rarely do.

In the larger cities, motorists often pull right onto the sidewalk to park. The law prohibits this, of course, and periodically the government embarks on campaigns to keep the sidewalks for pedestrians. Drivers, though, think that sidewalk parking makes sense, because the number of cars far surpasses the number of legal parking spots. They also know that the police have better things to do than issue traffic tickets.

Brazilians relax at a bar.

INTERMEDIARIES

Compromise is what keeps life going in Brazil; negotiation is the name of the game. Merchants and customers bargain over prices; taxi drivers and riders haggle over fares. While Brazilians take pride in their skills of negotiation, situations do occasionally arise that require outside help involving mediators.

Brazilian Catholics pray to patron saints, invoking them as allies. When they encounter a problem, they count on a saint to intercede with God on their behalf. The political equivalent to the saint is the colonel. He is the most influential citizen in rural communities, and people support the candidate he supports during elections, because they know he can get help from the elected person on their behalf.

Businessmen rely on a "fixer," called a *despachante* ("dehs-pah-SHAHN-cheh"), to deal with Brazil's relaxed attitude toward deadlines. The *despachantes* take care of routine everyday jobs. They might ask a relative who works for the trade ministry to speed up their employer's application for a license or an influential friend to make phone calls on behalf of their client. Brazilians dislike corruption, but it is a way of getting many things done.

FAMILY TIES

Bonds between friends and family are very tight in Brazil. Children usually live with their parents at least until they marry. If they do not earn enough to start out on their own, married children continue to live with their parents. Those who move out usually relocate close to home and visit their parents frequently.

Brazil has a social security system, but most of the elderly still depend on their children to support them. It is believed that having many children is the best guarantee against hardship in old age. For the poor, unfortunately, neither plan works. Unable to support all their children, many poor parents have no choice but to send them into the streets to find work. Brazil's cultural emphasis on family unity makes the problem with homeless children even more tragic.

Brazilians also stay in touch with relatives beyond their immediate family. While many young people in the United States have never met their second cousins, in Brazil distant cousins often meet at family gatherings and on a personal basis.

Godparents are very important in Brazil. A man who agrees to sponsor a child at baptism becomes a *padrinho* ("pah-DRIN-hoo") to the child and a *compadre* ("kom-PAH-dray") to the child's parents. The first word translates as "little father;" the second could be interpreted as "joint father." A godparent and his family become accepted members of the family of the baptized child, just as if they had married into the family.

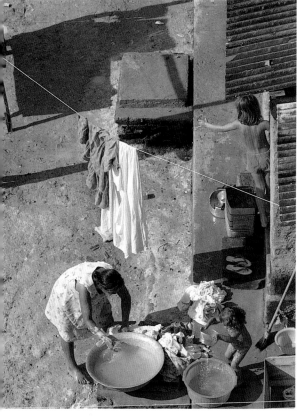

A mother does the laundry, while her toddler gets ready for a bath.

FRIENDSHIP

Brazilians have two kinds of friends. Social friends are people you get together with to eat, dance, or discuss local news, but not to share intimate subjects such as family problems or personal ambitions. Nor do social friends meet in one another's homes. The home is a private place reserved for family members and close friends. Only after many years of friendship can two Brazilians become close friends. The understanding and loyalty involved in this kind of friendship takes a long time to evolve. Most Brazilians have only a handful of close friends, whom they accept as family and whom they know they can count on in any crisis.

Duty demands that relatives and friends help one another in times of need, even if it causes a lot of inconvenience. A city dweller is bound to provide lodging for a visiting distant cousin, regardless of how long he or she stays. A host who suggests that the relative leave or pay rent would be considered rude and ungrateful. A good family member refuses to accept contributions from a visiting relative. To do so would be to reveal that he cannot fulfill his duty. Modern economics and values, however, are gradually changing this.

THE GATHERING OF FRIENDS

A Brazilian family of Japanese ancestry share with their guests a few drinks, laughs, and a plate of crabs.

A Brazilian family of Japanese ancestry share with their guests a few drinks, laughs, and a plate of crabs.

Brazilians love to be around other people. They enjoy chatting over drinks and dancing late into the night with friends. They love to have relatives and close friends stop by their homes.

A lot of drinking and conversation usually precedes the main meal whenever Brazilians hold dinner parties. Often, the host does not seat the guests until 11 P.M. At no time does the host leave the guests to attend to the preparation of the meal. To do so suggests a lack of respect or a sign of inadequate preparation for the guests' arrival. Where possible, servants are employed to prepare the meal; otherwise, the host should prepare everything in advance. Guests may bring a gift of flowers but never food, as the latter suggests that the host needs help entertaining friends.

To maintain the privacy of the home, most Brazilians hold large parties in clubs or community halls. Even parties for teenagers start late, often

after 10 P.M., and continue into the early morning hours.

Food, music, and dancing are standard ingredients of festivities. Guests may not necessarily have been invited. Brazilians think nothing of bringing friends or visiting relatives with them to parties. However, strangers should not expect to be introduced to anyone at the party. Formal introductions are considered too stiff for the festive atmosphere. You do not need to know someone's name in order to have a good conversation and a good time.

Brazilians place little emphasis on punctuality. They habitually show up late for both business and social functions. In fact, anyone arriving at a party earlier than half an hour after the time stated on the invitation is most likely to find an empty room. The earlybird may possibly even have arrived before the host. In the rare event that guests are expected to turn up on time, invitations specify the starting time as Swiss Time, British Time, or American Time.

A party in Rio de Janeiro.

The 15th birthday is a milestone in the life of any Brazilian girl. From then on, she is no longer treated as a girl but as a woman.

BIRTHDAYS Children's birthdays in Brazil are similar to those in the United States. Adults often have small family gatherings, followed by larger parties, to celebrate. Even casual friends make every effort to attend. To miss such an event is to fail in one's duty as a friend.

Upper-class families mark the 15th birthday of a daughter with a big debutante ball. The birthday girl and her closest friends dress in white gowns, and their escorts wear suits or tuxedos. The evening often begins with a Mass, then guests attend a reception, where a lavish buffet and live band await. At midnight, the guest of honor formally enters society by having one dance with her father, followed by a second with her escort.

WEDDINGS Before the wedding, the groom and his friends celebrate with a bachelor party at a club. The bridesmaids throw the bride a bridal shower in the kitchen of the bride's best friend's home.

The immediate family attends a small ceremony where civil documents are signed. The main event—the church wedding—then follows. All relatives and family friends attend the Mass and then a large reception. After cutting the wedding cake and bidding farewell to the guests, the newlyweds leave on their honeymoon.

FUNERALS Families usually bury their dead within 24 hours. News of the funeral travels by word of mouth, and those notified are expected to attend. Mourners stay up through the night, drinking and trading stories about the deceased.

At a designated time, a hearse carrying the coffin leads a procession to a church, where a requiem is offered. In smaller towns, the body will be buried in the church's private cemetery; in large cities, the procession moves to a larger public cemetery. A Mass is held in memory of the deceased after seven days, 30 days, and a year.

The proud and conservative *gauchos* epitomize Brazilian machismo.

MACHO MEN

Despite changing social trends, Brazil remains very much a man's country. The husband traditionally earns and manages his family's income, while the wife does the daily household chores and raises the children.

As do most South American men, Brazilian men always take the lead in courting the women. A man is expected to aggressively pursue the woman he has his eyes set on, but a woman who displays too much initiative in approaching men quickly gains a bad reputation.

A strict code of chivalry moderates the pursuit of love. Men are expected to give up their seats on buses and to open doors for women. In a restaurant, some men will seat their date, order for her, and pay the bill. Such small courtesies are important to the man, since they establish him as the woman's protector.

The main feature of male machismo is a desire to play a leading role and uphold one's honor. Brazilian men also do not feel compelled to act tough or hide their emotions. They do not hesitate to show affection to women, to hug close friends, or to cry over dying relatives.

THE GIRLS FROM IPANEMA

Brazilian women are famous around the world for their beauty and charm. "The Girl from Ipanema," made famous by a popular song of the 1960s, has become a representation of Latin beauty. Enchanted by a typical Brazilian beauty who frequented the famous Ipanema beach in Rio de Janeiro, songwriter Tom Jobim and a friend put their feelings to music and came up with a song that became a standard.

Natural Brazilian beauty.

Looking good is very important to Brazilian women, who seek to be stylish and charming in everything they do. They like to dress fashionably, always more fashionably than their male companions. Girls learn to wear jewelry and apply makeup from a young age. On the beach, they wear bathing suits that not only help them get a good tan, but also encourage them to keep trim.

While the machismo concept makes a man play a dominating role, Brazilian femininity promotes dependency on others. In the countryside, marriage is believed to be so essential for feminine self-fulfillment that single women in their 30s are pitied. Nonetheless, Brazilian women know how to get their way. While the men like to feel that they are in control, the women—with their twinkling eyes and gracious smiles—are experts at manipulating male egos.

WOMEN'S PLACE IN SOCIETY

Polite interaction between the sexes often plays out like a game. Men lavish attention on women, often leading up to romantic propositions. Women smile at their suitors, chat with them, and appreciate the attention. But they rarely yield to an advance.

The flirting sometimes crosses a fine line and fuels masculine jealousy, exposing a double standard in the Brazilian attitude toward marriage. Society, and women, quietly tolerate extramarital affairs by married men. Many even accept such infidelity as the inevitable result of machismo. But each year, hundreds of wives are beaten, and even killed, because of their husbands' jealousy and suspicions. Women rarely report these actions, since the law rarely punishes men for "crimes of passion."

Fortunately, this is slowly changing. Brazil is gradually overturning such attitudes. Stricter laws have been passed for crimes committed against wives. A growing number of women are pursuing careers and participating in activities previously regarded as unfeminine, such as team sports and politics.

Like in many other cultures, social trends in Brazil are building toward gender equality.

In 1997, Brazil began a system reserving 30 percent of the membership of each political party for women. Yet there remains a long way to go in achieving gender equality in Brazilian politics. Although women make up the majority of the electorate, few run for public office and few of those who do run actually get elected. In the 2000 municipal elections, women made up less than eight percent of the almost 15,000 mayoral candidates and won in less than six percent of the cities.

BRINGING UP CHILDREN

Having a large family and being frequently visited by relatives, Brazilian children are constantly surrounded by loved ones and never left alone. Many families hire nurses to look after the children, and those who cannot afford nurses can always count on help from their relatives.

Babies in particular receive constant attention. They rarely escape the hands of the caregiver, and when they cry they become the center of attention. Sometimes even strangers on the street will stop to offer suggestions to a mother with a crying baby.

Junior takes a bath in his miniature tub under the watchful eyes of his siblings.

Many Brazilian parents pamper their children. Few believe in strict discipline. They may simply send a child out of the room for bad behaviour when there are guests, but they usually ignore a child who acts up in church or in a store. They believe it is inevitable that children will get bored or unhappy in a place where there is nothing to entertain them.

Until they reach the teenage years, children rarely do work around the house. Also, upper-class Brazilians do not allow their schooling children to work part-time, as they feel that such work suggests to outsiders that the family is in financial trouble. In any case, Brazilian law does not allow children to work until they reach 16 years of age.

In this male-oriented society, boys are treated more leniently than girls. Girls usually cannot stay out late, and their parents do not like them going out without a chaperone. Their parents also take more interest in their friends than in their brother's friends. Teenagers usually start dating at around age 17. First dates are not seen as anything serious, since newly dating couples often go out in groups.

EDUCATION

Students in Brazil attend eight years of elementary school and three years of high school. Because many poor teenagers have part-time jobs and because of a shortage of classroom space, many high schools hold classes in shifts. Progress is measured in classroom hours rather than school years, so that working students can learn at their own pace. Although student enrollment in schools has risen sharply over the past two decades, many children from lower-income families stop going to school after 10 years of age.

Uniformed schoolchildren in João Pessoa.

Every January, thousands of 18-year-olds crowd into lecture halls, gymnasiums, and even soccer stadiums to take the *vestibular* ("vehs-tee-boo-LAHR"), the examination that determines whether they will be admitted to a university.

Public and private universities give different entrance exams for different schools in the university. Students who want to study nutrition or biology must take two different exams; if they want to apply to two private and a public institution, they have to take six exams. Once admitted as biology students, they cannot switch to nutrition without taking the *vestibular* again.

Tuition fees are very low for those who pass, thanks to support from the government. College students are a select group: only one in 100 children who enroll in the first grade ever goes to college. About 80 percent of Brazil's adult population is literate. Secondary education has been restructured to emphasize practical arts and scientific knowledge.

RELIGION

NINETY PERCENT OF BRAZILIANS are Roman Catholic, making Brazil the world's largest Catholic nation. However, the Catholicism practiced in Brazil has been strongly influenced by local cultures and beliefs.

On New Year's Eve in Rio de Janeiro, women dressed in white march across the beach and into the sea, carrying a statue of the Virgin Mary. They launch miniature boats carrying flowers and perfume. If the boats make it out to sea, it means that their offerings have been accepted by the Virgin Mary. If they wash to shore, then they have been rejected. On the third Thursday of January in Salvador da Bahia, women dressed in colorful clothing scrub the steps leading to the Church of Nosso Senhor do Bonfim. In the "miracle room" of this church, hundreds of wax models of human limbs are displayed as tokens of thanks by the faithful who believe they were healed by Nosso Senhor do Bonfim, or Our Lord of the Good Ending.

In October in Belém, thousands join a procession leading a statue of Our Lady of Nazareth through the city streets. They hold on to a thick rope several blocks long, which is used to pull the carriage bearing the statue. They believe that Our Lady of Nazareth will answer their prayers for helping her along the streets.

The same month, in Rio de Janeiro, thousands of faithful get down on their knees and climb 365 steps leading up to the Church of Our Lady of the Cliff. They do this to atone for their sins or to express gratitude for favors received.

Opposite: **This huge statue of Jesus Christ in Rio de Janeiro has become a world-famous landmark.**

Below: **The interior of Brasília's magnificent cathedral.**

FOLK RELIGION

The ceremonies Brazilian Catholics celebrate show the influence of African and, to a lesser extent, indigenous Indian religions. The New Year's Eve festival is dedicated not to the Virgin Mary, but to Iemanja, the African goddess of the sea. Missionaries started Belém's annual procession in 1763 as a way to attract Amazon Indians to Christianity.

Candles surround offerings on a colorful mat— the trademark symbols of a *Macumba* ritual.

Catholic priests arrived in Brazil with the early colonizers and set out to convert the Indians and, later, the African slaves. They achieved partial success: their pupils became Catholics in name, but molded their new religion to fit old spiritual practices. The missionaries could do little about this because of their small numbers. To this day, Brazil suffers from a shortage of priests.

The shortage of priests has acutely impacted the religious practices of the poor. Left to their own devices, the poor developed their own form of folk Catholicism. They adopted some elements of Indian religions, such as asking medicine men to heal sicknesses, and some elements of European folklore, such as the belief in wolfmen.

Of all the non-Christian religions, the African ones were the most influential. Brazilians took on African gods called *orixás* ("oh-ree-SHAHS") and gave them Christian names. Oxala came to be represented by Jesus Christ, popularly known as Nosso Senhor do Bonfim. Ogun, a hunter god, and Xango, a god of lightning, took on the identities of Saints Anthony and George. Iemanja is, as we have seen, portrayed as the Virgin Mary. Saints Jerome, Cosmos, Damian, Barbara, Anna, and many others inherited the identities of African *orixás*.

Some worshipers view saints to be almost as important as the Virgin Mary or even Jesus Christ. To many, the main concern is not salvation or life after death so much as surviving in this world. They pray to the saints, who they believe are capable of bestowing favors upon those who revere them. Saint Anthony, for example, can help single women find husbands, Saint Blas protects against sore throats, and Saint Lucia heals the blind.

To win a saint's favor, believers make promises. They may promise to climb the steps of a church on their knees or to wash the church. If a saint cures them of an affliction, they may make a pilgrimage to the saint's shrine to offer a model of their healed limb or organ. In larger cities, processions honoring different saints are common. Every town organizes a procession on the feast day of its patron saint. One survey showed that the Brazilian Catholic Church organizes more than 37,000 processions annually—over 100 each day!

Nowadays, it is impossible to distinguish between traditional Catholics and folk Catholics. Every Brazilian Catholic accepts some folk beliefs. In general, however, the difference follows economic lines: the upper class adheres to traditional Catholic beliefs more than the poor do, with the middle class somewhere in between.

71

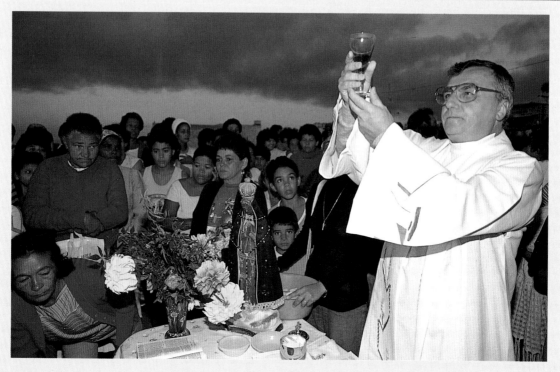

THE CHURCH'S SOCIAL ROLE

While they have always been few in number, Catholic priests have played an important role throughout Brazil's history in working for the well-being of the masses.

Jesuit priests arrived with the earliest colonizers and provided education for the settlers and the Indians. They also fought vigorously to protect the Indians from slavery, until their efforts caused the Portuguese king to expel them from Brazil in 1759.

During the colonial period, priests began to establish lay brotherhoods, some of which still exist today. These organizations played the role of a social security agency. They provided help for elderly or sick members and built numerous hospitals, orphanages, and churches.

Today, Brazilian priests have taken a leading role in pushing for aid to indigenous Indians, landless peasants, and the poor. The National Council of Brazilian Bishops has said that the Church should not support political parties, but should strive to promote the fair use of land and fair treatment of workers.

Radical priests accept the doctrine of liberation theology, which combines Marxism and Christianity. They believe that a struggle by the poor working class is needed to carry out God's plan. Liberation theology shows the extremes to which some priests have taken their role as agents of social change.

AFRICAN RELIGIONS

African rituals still thrive in Brazil, particularly among the poor. Carried out secretly at night in special ceremonial houses, they play a part in preserving Afro-Brazilian heritage. The priest or priestess who directs these rites can often tell the story of his or her ancestors, going back to the time when they left Africa in slave ships.

However, these African religions have been influenced by European and Indian practices. Many non-blacks have been accepted as members of these cults. Social status rather than ethnicity is the criterion for membership. If active members should earn enough to rise into the middle or upper classes, their new social position will probably force them to quit.

Cults introduced from West Africa are the roots from which most Brazilian rituals evolved. In Africa, these cults centered around the ceremonial preparation of an object known as a "fetish," which supposedly held supernatural powers. In Brazil, the fetish has given way to the powers of the *orixás*, or gods. A pantheon of *orixás* existed in Africa, but they took on a larger role in Brazil, where they were associated with Catholic figures.

Candomblé ("kahn-dohm-BLEH") and *macumba* ("mah-KOOM-bah"), the two main cults, reflect the varying degrees of outside influence on African religions. *Candomblé*, practiced mainly in Salvador da Bahia, has stayed closer to its West African roots. *Macumba*, practiced mostly in Rio de Janeiro, brings beliefs from West and South Africa together with European beliefs.

Hundreds of colorful boats accompany thousands of people on shore escorting a statue of Jesus during the celebration of the Feast of the Lord Jesus of the Navigators. Most of the coastal northeast joins Salvador in this celebration.

CANDOMBLÉ A *pai de santo* ("pah-ee deh SAHN-teh"), or father of the saint, or *mai de santo* ("mah-ee deh SAHN-teh"), or mother of the saint, presides over a *candomblé* ritual; both men and women are allowed to serve. The inner circle of devotees are the *filhos de santo* ("FEE-loos deh SAHN-teh"), or children of the saint. In Bahia, these are usually young women who undergo a complicated initiation ritual to reach this stage.

For a period of up to one year, the *filhos de santo* must remain inside the ceremonial house of their *pai de santo*, eating a set diet and observing a strict set of rules. When this is completed, they are bathed in water spiced with scented leaves, after which the blood of a sacrificed animal is poured over their heads.

The main *candomblé* ritual is the giving of a meal to the *orixás*. On set dates, the *pai de santo* prepares a fetish for a designated god. The fetish for each *orixá* must be prepared differently. For Xango, whose fetish is a

Candomblé believers link hands during a beach ceremony in Rio de Janeiro.

stone, he will place the stone in a basin, surround it with palm oil and sacred leaves, and then spill the blood of a sacrificed rooster over it. The *pai de santo* places the fetish in a special worship room. Followers crowd around the room, with one side reserved for a band of drummers. The *pai de santo* stands in the center, surrounded by the *filhos de santo*.

Several small initial offerings are made to different *orixás*, always starting with the evil spirit named Exu. It is believed that an early gift to this god prevents his interference in later offerings.

Accompanied by the thumping of the drums, the *filhos de santo* dance and sing invocations to different *orixás*. Hours pass, the rhythm of the drumbeat gets faster, the dancing becomes more frenzied, and emotions build up. The climax comes when an *orixá* possesses the spirit of one of the dancers. The entranced *filho de santo* begins to shake uncontrollably until she collapses. When she revives, the *pai de santo* gives her the symbol of the *orixá* who visited her soul, and she continues to dance. Those present revere the *orixá* in her and ask favors of it. During the ceremony, which may last all night, several *orixás* will make their presence known.

Candomblé priests and priestesses preside over a ceremony. Leading *candomblé* priestesses are said to be able to tell the names of their ancestors as far back as when their ancestors were still in Africa. Before these priestesses die, they pass on their knowledge to their understudies, who will memorize by heart the entire family tree.

Bahian women and girls take a breather after an exhausting *macumba* ceremony.

MACUMBA Followers of *macumba* appeal to a wider array of spirits. This cult combines elements of *candomblé* with the ancestral worship brought to Brazil by slaves from the south of Africa and with the European philosophy of spiritualism. According to this philosophy, the living can communicate with the souls of the dead.

The *macumba* and *candomblé* rites are similar, but the spirits that possess *macumba* dancers are not always *orixás*. It is believed they may represent a natural force, some god, or an ancestor of one of the followers. The spirits sometimes speak to those present through the voice of the possessed *filho de santo*. Just as often, it is believed fun-loving spirits just want to use their hosts as the means to drink, dance, smoke, and have a good time. Special *macumba* ceremonies focus solely on healing. In these, only the *pai de santo* becomes entranced. Possessed by the appropriate spirit, he is believed to be able to cure afflictions simply by blowing cigar smoke over his patient or brushing feathers over the wounded area.

RURAL MIRACLE WORKERS

A different type of religion flourishes in the harsh conditions of Brazil's northeast. Dry weather makes life difficult for the farmers in this region, so they are understandably drawn to preachers who herald the end of this world and the beginning of a new, more just society.

Over the years, many such ministers have won the reputation of being miracle workers. The two most famous ones drew large numbers of followers in the late 19th century. Even today, these rural miracle workers in the northeast are revered as saints.

ANTÔNIO CONSELHEIRO Antônio Maciel, who became known as Antônio Conselheiro, or Antônio the Counselor, began preaching in the 1870s. He believed that the world would come to an end by 1899, when King Sebastian would appear in Brazil to bring justice to all. This 16th-century Portuguese king had disappeared during a Holy Crusade to North Africa, and many people at that time regarded him as a savior who would reappear to end injustice.

Conselheiro gained a reputation as a miracle worker and soon found himself thronged by followers. He also found himself in trouble when the army overthrew Dom Pedro II in 1889.

Brazil's new government did not like him, since he had always taught those who listened to him that an emperor ruled by divine right. The army sent four expeditions against New Jerusalem, the city Conselheiro had built in Bahia as his base. The first three failed, but the fourth, in 1897, destroyed the town and its leader. According to legend, only a child, an old man, and two wounded men survived. The world did end for Conselheiro and his followers, but myths about him live on in the northeast today.

African slaves in Brazil were forced by their Catholic masters to give up their African religions. But instead of abandoning their gods completely, the slaves just gave the African gods Christian names. Iemanja, the goddess of rivers and water, came to be represented by the Virgin Mary, the queen of the heavens and seas. Oxala, the most powerful African god of fertility and harvests, came to be represented by Jesus Christ. Exu, a wicked spirit, came to be represented by Satan.

FATHER CICERO A contemporary of Conselheiro, Father Cicero, a priest from the state of Ceara, fared better. He lives on after death as a religious icon and an object of worship.

He first became popular because of his compassion for the poor. But he became famous in 1890 because of the "miracle of the host." During a Mass that year, a woman who received Holy Communion from him immediately collapsed to the floor with blood dripping from her mouth. Believers claimed the host had physically turned into the flesh and blood of Jesus Christ.

Skeptics claimed that sickness made the woman cough up blood, so the local bishop sent in investigators. His team concluded that no miracle had taken place, and the Church eventually excommunicated Father Cicero, but this did not hurt his popularity.

The people of the northeast believed the priest had magical powers. They saved everything he touched, from his clipped fingernails to the water he used to wash his clothes. When Father Cicero died in 1934, he was one of the most influential men in Brazil.

He is still revered today. A 75-foot (23-m) statue of him stands in the town of Juazeiro do Norte, where thousands arrive each year to visit his grave. Shops all over the northeast sell images of Father Cicero, and many Brazilians pray to him for favors. Some people believe he has not died but will return soon to herald the coming of a new age.

Opposite: **A giant statue of Father Cicero in Juazeiro do Norte. Cicero was considered a sort of savior who would one day magically make the dry lands of the northeast flourish like beautiful gardens and stop poverty and hunger.**

Below: **The sale of religious images is a thriving business in Brazil.**

LANGUAGE

BRAZIL IS THE ONLY LATIN AMERICAN COUNTRY where the national language is Portuguese. Like other countries of North and South America, Brazil inherited its language from European colonizers.

Opposite: **Most newsstand items in Brazil are printed in Portuguese.**

BRAZILIAN PORTUGUESE

As the English spoken in the United States differs in some ways from that spoken in England, so has Brazil's Portuguese developed a character of its own. Educated citizens of Brazil and Portugal can still communicate and have a fruitful conversation once they adjust to each other's accents. Working-class Brazilians, however, would have a hard time understanding Portuguese speakers in Europe.

The difference between the two stems mostly from the influence of Brazil's Indians. The early colonists survived by trading with these Indians, so they had to learn to communicate with them. For the first 200 years of Brazil's history, an Indian language called Tupi-Guarani was used more than Portuguese.

Today, Tupi-Guarani survives only among a few Indian groups living near the border with Paraguay, but it left its mark on Brazilian Portuguese. One researcher compiled a list of 20,000 Portuguese words with Indian origins, making up about one-sixth of the total Portuguese vocabulary. Portuguese settlers borrowed most Indian words to name unfamiliar animals and plants. Some of the names, such as *manioc* and *jaguar*, have even found their way into the English language.

Other outside influences have flavored Brazil's Portuguese. In Bahia and Rio de Janeiro, Brazilians speak with a flowing, almost musical rhythm. Many attribute this to the African heritage of the states. The vocabulary and cadence in some southern towns, in turn, reflect the influence of German, Italian, and Spanish immigrants.

ALPHABETS AND ACCENTS

The Portuguese alphabet has three fewer letters than the English alphabet has. In everyday Brazilian Portuguese conversation, the letters "k," "w," and "y" of the English alphabet appear only in foreign names.

The 23 letters of the Portuguese alphabet are pronounced much the way they are in English, except for the letter "x," which sounds like "sh." For example, the name "Xingu" is pronounced "Shingu."

As in English, "c" can have a hard or soft sound. When it is annotated with a cedilla, appearing as "ç," it is pronounced softly. For example, *açucar*, meaning "sugar," is pronounced "ah-SOO-kahr."

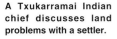

A Txukarramai Indian chief discusses land problems with a settler.

Portuguese makes extensive use of accent marks. All five vowels take the acute (´) and grave (`) accents. In addition, *a*, *e*, and *o* sometimes take the circumflex (^). The diaeresis (¨) sometimes appears on *i* and *u*, while the tilde (~) is used with *a* and *o*.

Unaccented Portuguese words are usually stressed on the starting syllable if they end in "a," "e," or "o" sounds. Otherwise, the emphasis falls on the final syllable. For example, *casa*, meaning "house," is pronounced "KAH-zah," while *casar*, meaning "to marry," is pronounced "kah-ZAHR."

NAMES

In general, Brazilians are warm and friendly and love good conversation in a cheerful atmosphere. At the same time, they are very aware of the codes of social standing and are careful to show proper respect at all times with people they talk to. The manner in which they address one another reflects both the formal and informal sides of their personalities.

FORMAL NAMES Brazilians only use "you" when speaking to close friends, children, and those from the lower classes. With senior citizens, casual acquaintances, and strangers, they use *o senhor*, meaning "the gentleman," or *a senhora*, meaning "the lady." Instead of asking "How are you today?" they ask "How is the lady (or gentleman) today?"

Brazilians often bestow further honorary titles on wealthier or better-educated citizens. Just because someone is called Colonel da Silva does not necessarily mean he is a military officer. Likewise, Doctor da Silva may not be a physician, just a prosperous merchant who knows how to read and conjugate verbs in the subjunctive tense. This is particularly true in rural towns where most people are illiterate. Those who can decipher official documents have a place of honor in the community.

Portuguese is the language of instruction in schools in Brazil.

COUNTING TO 10 THE INDIAN WAY

When the Portuguese first arrived in Brazil, they found Indians speaking a number of different languages. Few of these dialects still exist today. If Brazilian children spoke the language of the Kayapo Indians who live in the Xingu National Park, they would count to 10 like this:

1	pudi
2	amaikrut
3	amaikrutikeke
4	amaikrutamaikrut
5	amaikrutamaikrutikeke
6	amaikrutamaikrutamaikrut
7	amaikrutamaikrutamaikrutikeke
8	amaikrutamaikrutamaikrutamaikrut
9	amaikrutamaikrutamaikrutamaikrutikeke
10	amaikrutamaikrutamaikrutamaikrutamaikrut

INFORMAL NAMES In general, knowing someone's full name is not as important in Brazil as it is in the United States or Europe. Often, introductions will not be made when a Brazilian brings a friend to a party. Doing so adds an air of formality to a friendly setting. If an introduction is made, only the first name or nickname is given.

Another reason for this is that Brazilians often do not know the last name of their friends. Most Brazilians are known by either their first or last name, but not both. A teacher named Carlos Mattos would be called Professor Carlos by his students and Senhor Carlos by his colleagues. His close friends would simply call him Carlos, but many of those who know him would not know his last name.

Brazilians often use names that do not appear on their birth certificates. Adults often christen young children with nicknames that last a lifetime. Brazil's most famous soccer player, known to his countrymen and to the world as Pelé, is really Edson Arantes de Nascimento. Two top players on Brazil's 1990 World Cup soccer team go by the names Careca, meaning "bald man," and Alemão, meaning "German." This practice is not limited to sports stars.

Brazilians know Luis Inacio da Silva, the leader of the Worker's Party and the runner-up in the 1989 presidential elections, as Lula. Brazilian children know the folk story about Lampeão, a famous bandit of the northeast. But few children recognize him by his full name, Virgulino Ferreira. Brazil's most famous sculptor is known as Aleijadinho, which means "the little cripple."

BODY LANGUAGE

Actions speak louder than words when Brazilians greet one another. For a business contact or new acquaintance, a handshake suffices, perhaps with a pat on the back if the setting is informal.

But a meeting of friends calls for something more. Two men exchange an *abraço* ("ah-BRAH-soo"), a firm hug, while women trade *beijinhos* ("bay-JIN-hoos"), kisses on the cheek. By custom, a married woman receives a kiss on each side of the face, but a single woman gets an extra kiss. If it does not come, she is liable to say, "Give me three so that I won't be an old maid!" When men and women meet, they are slightly more restrained, but relatives and friends still trade one or two *beijinhos*.

As this custom shows, physical contact is more common in Brazil than in the United States. Foreigners often feel uncomfortable about how close Brazilians stand in conversation and about the way they grab or touch the arm to emphasize a point.

Brazilians, in turn, do not understand why Americans do things like excuse themselves when squeezing through a crowd, for example. To Brazilians, brushing by to get out of an elevator or nudging someone to the side with the touch of the hand requires no apology or excuse.

Yanomami Indians in an invitation talk. The messenger of the guest party embraces the headman of the host party.

TALKING WITH THE HANDS

Brazilians are uninhibited when they talk. Good conversation means loud voices and lots of gestures. From the Brazilian point of view, people who talk with a level voice, keeping their hands by their side appear to not really believe what they are saying. Here are a few Brazilian hand gestures.

BRUSHING THE FINGERTIPS This is a versatile gesture. You shake your hands back and forth so that the fingertips of one hand brush against those of the other. This usually means "I don't care" or "It doesn't matter." Asked how he is doing, a bored man may respond with this gesture and a shoulder shrug to indicate that things are as usual, not too good and not too bad.

KISSING THE FINGERTIPS "Everything's great!" This is shown by holding all five fingers of one hand up to the mouth, kissing them, then opening up the hand as you fling it forward. This gesture is also used to express appreciation for a beautiful painting or woman.

FINGER SNAP One of the most common gestures is to make a snapping sound with the fingers. Holding thumb and middle finger together, the Brazilian relaxes the hand and shakes it so that the index finger whips against the middle finger. Brazilian children learn this at an early age, but foreigners have a hard time

Brushing the fingertips

Kissing the fingertips

picking it up. Brazilians snap their fingers so often it is impossible to assign a precise meaning to the gesture. They snap their fingers to indicate pain, to tell friends to hurry up, or to show appreciation for a joke. If children disobey their parents, their friends snap their fingers as if to say, "Boy, are you in trouble now!"

FINGER UNDER THE EYE When an American finds something hard to believe, he or she may exclaim, "In a pig's eye!" Brazilians indicate disbelief by pointing to the eye with a knowing grin and gently pulling down the skin beneath the eye. They may emphasize the point by saying, "*Aqui, oh!*" ("ah-KEE, oh"), meaning "Sure, right here!"

FINGERS POINTING UP "I can't take it anymore!" Holding the fingers together with hands pointing upward means you have had enough. Brazilians also use this gesture when talking about a crowded place.

OTHER GESTURES Brazilians show a clenched fist to accuse someone of being a miser without calling the person a *pão duro* ("pow DOO-roh"), or "hard piece of bread." When Brazilians hold the thumb and index finger together at the mouth and motion drinking from a cup, you know they are saying "Let's have a drink." To show approval or to indicate that everything is all right, Brazilians give the thumbs-up.

Finger under the eye

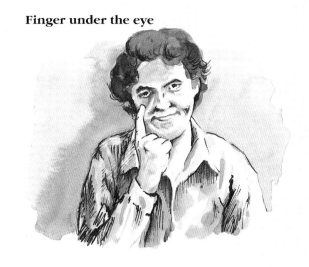

Fingers pointing up

ARTS

MORE THAN ANY OTHER ART FORM, Brazil's music best captures the nation's heritage. Brazilian music developed from the blending of European, African, and indigenous Indian roots.

The first Jesuit missionaries in Brazil discovered that ritual chanting accompanied by rattles and panpipes played a key role in the religious rites of the indigenous Indians. These missionaries then taught the Indians the Catholic Mass using Gregorian chants. This Indian tradition still survives in the *caboclinho* ("kah-boh-KLEEN-hoo"), a folk dance of Brazil's northeast. Dressed in Indian outfits, the entourage marches in two columns. A chief recites passages, finishing each line on a low note, and the other dancers respond with a set chorus. A three-man band accompanies the entourage, one man playing the flute, another the *reco-reco* ("HEH-koh HEH-koh"), and the third a drum. Each man reinforces the beat by using a bow and arrow as rhythm sticks.

Music and dance also played an essential role in the rites of the African slaves. The colonists considered the slaves' dances wild and obscene and tried to suppress them. Plantation owners, on the other hand, appreciated the musical skills of their slaves and taught them to play European instruments. Bands of slaves provided the music when owners entertained. Gradually, African rhythms and instruments found their way into mainstream music. By the early 1800s, colonial barons and ladies in elegant salons found themselves dancing the *lundu* ("loon-DHUH"), then still regarded as a primitive, lascivious dance. Today's samba is a direct descendant of the *lundu*.

At the same time, the slaves learned to appreciate European instruments such as the accordion, tambourine, and guitar. These instruments still form the backbone of Brazil's music. The Africans adapted these to their style and incorporated some European rhythms and harmonies.

Opposite: **A craftsman outside a church carves a holy image in a piece of wood.**

The beat of the *surdo* often provides the rhythm for the samba.

THE NATIONAL BEAT

Today, just as European, African, and Indian heritages have mixed to produce countless ethnic variations in Brazil, so have these cultures combined to produce an incredible array of music and dance styles. Of the many categories of music in Brazil, the most famous is the samba.

Samba is the national beat, but there are many different types of samba. *Samba do morro* ("SAHM-bah duh MOH-hoh"), or hill samba, refers to samba played by a large group using only percussion instruments.

In Carnival parades, the samba schools play *samba enredo* ("ehn-HEH-doh"), or theme samba, with a lead singer and a chorus accompanying the percussion band. Small groups in nightclubs perform *samba canção* ("kahn-SAH-oo"), or samba song, and *samba de salão* ("deh SAH-lah-oo"), or parlor samba. To a samba beat, the lead vocalist may croon a romantic song of love or make a sarcastic commentary on local politics.

Samba de roda ("deh ROH-dah"), or circle samba, is the traditional slave dance, where participants sit in a circle with only one person dancing in the middle. The dancers take turns in the middle. When they finish their turn, they designate the next dancer by standing in front of that person and thrusting their hips forward.

In a *samba rural* ("HOO-rah-oo"), also called *samba paulista* ("pah-hoo-LEES-tah"), dancers line up in two rows, while in a *samba lençol* ("lehn-SOHL"), or sheet samba, couples dance in step.

As with ethnic descriptions, most Brazilians have little time for detailed musical terminology. Whether the sound comes from a costumed percussion section parading along the street or from a lone guitarist accompanied by a friend drumming hands on a table, a Brazilian need only hear it to know that it is samba music.

BUMBA-MEU-BOI

Portuguese colonists brought several dramatic folk dances called *folguedos* ("fohl-GAY-doos") to Brazil. Usually performed during religious festivals, many survive to this day. The *congada* ("cohng-GAH-deh") reenacts a battle of the Crusades between Christians and Moors, while the *cavalhada* ("kah-val-LEE-ah-dah") mimics a medieval jousting competition.

The *bumba-meu-boi* ("boom-bah may-AH-boy"), the most common surviving dance, is typically Brazilian. Folk groups around the country perform it during the Christmas season. The dance centers on the death and resurrection of a bull. Some people consider it a parody of a bullfight, while others believe its origin lies in the rites of pagan religions that worshiped the bull as a symbol of power and fertility.

The plot usually has a cowboy named Mateus trying to sell a bull to a wealthy rancher. The bull attacks the crowd that surrounds it, is stabbed with a knife, and dies. Mateus, however, revives it using folk medicine.

Brazilians today are not really concerned about the story or its symbolism. The *bumba-meu-boi* is now mainly a festive occasion, filled with bright costumes and lively music and dance. Witty exchanges between the soloists and the chorus add elements of humor and social commentary.

The star of the dance is the bull. One man plays the part, bearing on his shoulders a bull-shaped wooden framework covered with velvet. Authentic bull's horns, elegant stitching, ribbons, and sometimes even colorful semiprecious stones decorate the cloth.

Always the center of attention, the bull attacks then retreats, shudders in the throes of death, then bounces back to life. In the end, it breaks out of the circle of dancers and leads a festive procession through the streets.

The *bumba-meu-boi* is generally seen as the comic representation of Portugal's non-lethal bullfights. This very rhythmic and colorful dance is performed most authentically in the northeastern states of Brazil.

91

MUSICAL INSTRUMENTS

EUROPEAN INSTRUMENTS The Portuguese contributed an array of stringed instruments to Brazil's music. The Portuguese guitar, the *viola* ("vee-OH-lah"), was the favorite instrument of Iberian musicians as far back as the 13th century. This 10-string instrument is gradually giving way to the modern six-string guitar, but it is still an essential part of Brazilian folk music.

The *cavaquinho* ("kah-vah-KEEN-uh"), a small guitar similar to a Hawaiian ukelele, the *bandolim* ("bahn-doh-LEEM"), which is a mandolin, and the *rabeca* ("hah-BEH-kah"), a Portuguese fiddle, live on as well. Virtuoso performers on these instruments come together to play a lively acoustic style Brazilians call *choro* ("SHOH-roh") music.

The accordion, tambourine, and the triangle all came to Brazil from Europe. So did the *tarol* ("tah-ROHL") and the *surdo* ("SOOR-doh"). The *tarol* is a small drum similar to those used in marching bands, while the *surdo* is a large bass drum.

Brazilian street musicians drum up a beat accompanied by the accordion and tambourine.

AFRICAN INSTRUMENTS Brazil inherited numerous instruments from Africa, including the unique *cuica* ("koo-EE-kah"), which produces a most unusual squeal. A narrow rod fastened to the middle of the drumhead extends through the hollow cylinder of the *cuica*. Musicians rub a damp cloth along this rod. The friction causes the leather skin to vibrate, creating a high-pitched sound, something like the noise a damp cloth makes when rubbed against a window. By pressing their fingers at different points along the drumhead and varying the speed at which they rub the rod, the musicians can control the noise the *cuica* makes.

Another African import is the *tamborim* ("tahm-boor-IM"), a small drum the size of a tambourine that does not have metallic discs and is not meant to be shaken. Samba masters usually hold it in one hand while drumming it with a small baton.

Another popular instrument is the *reco-reco*, a term used to describe a frog's croak. A stick is scraped along the carved notches of the wooden instrument to produce a similar sound.

The *berimbau* ("bee-rim-BOW") also makes a unique sound. With one wire tied between the ends of a slightly curved stick, it looks like an archer's bow. Master players twang the wire by hitting it with a stick. They vary the note by using their free hand to tighten or loosen the wire. A gourd attached to the bottom of the *berimbau* acts as a resonator. The musician holds it against his stomach to start, then changes the timbre of the sound by moving it to and from his body. The *berimbau* is today used exclusively to accompany *capoeira* ("cah-poh-EE-rah"), an African martial arts dance featuring exotic leaps and kicks.

Iaualapiti Indians play their sacred flutes during a festival. Their music has little melody but complex rhythms. Indian contributions to popular music include percussion instruments, the nasal tone in song, the one-word chorus, and the ending of a verse on a lower note.

INDIAN INSTRUMENTS Rattles and pipes were the preferred instruments of Brazil's Indians. Some Indian groups in the Amazon still bring out the *urua* ("OO-roo-ah") for formal ceremonies. It takes a barrel-chested Indian with above-average lung capacity to blow music out of this 10-foot-long (3-m-long) pipe. Simpler and more common is the *pife* ("peef"), a simple bamboo flute still popular among the poor in the north and northeast. The standard Indian rattle is the *maraca* ("mah-RAH-kah"), a hollow gourd with a wooden handle partially filled with dried seeds. Africans also brought rattles with them to the new world, so scholars can only guess the origin of the several varieties used in Brazil.

Art lovers view an exhibition on Avenida Rio Branco in Rio de Janeiro, with the Municipal Theater in the background. Located in the area are two other impressive buildings: the National Library, which hosts both neoclassical and modern art, and the Museum of Fine Arts, which displays the works of Brazil's greatest artists.

POPULAR ART

Popular art flourishes in open-air markets called *feiras* ("FAY-rahs"). In the rural towns of the interior, the *feiras* are big events. Vendors sell everything from chickens to pots and pans to carved nativity sets to cotton clothing. In larger cities, the *feiras* focus more on popular art than on daily essentials.

Good luck charms are another bestseller. Tiny fruit and animal figures created by silversmiths in Bahia are said to represent *candomblé* spirits. People wear a *balangandã* ("bah-lahng-gahn-DAH"), a cluster of such figures on a chain, believing it has the power to ward off evil spirits.

Another charm is the *figa* ("FEE-gah"), a model of a clenched fist where the thumb sticks out between the index and middle fingers. While the origin of this symbol is unknown, many Brazilians wear it to fend off the "evil eye." Artisans sell *figa* in all sizes, made from wood, silver, or semiprecious stones.

Many artists run shops near churches dedicated to popular saints. They specialize in creating *ex votos* ("ehs VOH-toos"), items that Catholics offer to repay saints for favors granted. Such an item could be a clay model of a broken leg that is healing or an elaborate painting of a saint's miraculous intercession in a car crash.

Along the São Francisco River, sculptors carve *carrancas* ("kah-HAN-kahs"), half-human, half-beast creatures, with glaring eyes and sharp teeth.

LITERATURE

Brazilian literature accounts for half of all literary publications in Latin America.

Brazil's post-independence literature described the country's forests, the Indians, the African slaves, and urban activities. The best-known poets of this period included Gonçalves Dias (1823–1864), Castro Alves (1847–1871), and José de Alencar (1829–1877).

The novels of Joaquim Manuel de Macedo (1820–1882) and Alfredo d'Escragnolle Taunay (1843–1899) are still widely read in Brazil. José Américo de Almeida (1887–1969) and Jorge Amado (b. 1902) wrote about the problems of life in the northeast. Amado wrote his first novels on cocoa plantation workers in Bahia and fishermen in coastal villages. These works have been translated into 33 languages. In the 1950s, Amado wrote several internationally acclaimed novels.

Brazil's most innovative writer was perhaps João Guimarães Rosa (1908–1967). He has been credited for creating, through his novels, a new style of writing, almost a new language.

The *carranca*, a figure-head on boats in the São Francisco River. The river is said to have a history of evil spirits, including the "Water Bitch," "Water Monster," and "Backwoodsman of the Water," who have sunk many ships in the past. The *carranca* is there to scare these monsters away.

The Last Supper, sculpted by Aleijadinho and his students.

"THE LITTLE CRIPPLE"

Brazil's most famous sculptor is also one of the world's most remarkable artists. Antônio Francisco Lisboa, born around 1740, became known as Aleijadinho, "the little cripple."

Aleijadinho was struck by an unconfirmed disease—perhaps leprosy or arthritis—in the prime of his life. The disease paralyzed his hands, but not his passion and determination. He tied a hammer and a chisel to his wrists and continued to work.

Aleijadinho amazingly managed to complete 12 remarkable life-sized soapstone statues of Old Testament biblical prophets and the 66 woodcarvings that make up the Stations of the Cross in the town of Congonhas do Campo near Belo Horizonte.

The illegitimate son of a Portuguese architect and a slave, Aleijadinho received no formal education during his 80 years, and he never set eyes on the ocean. Yet his masterpieces are considered among the finest of baroque art anywhere in the world. He learned about the European baroque style from books and missionaries.

Aleijadinho's statue of Christ.

Along with his sculptures, Aleijadinho designed many beautiful churches, each with trademark large, rounded bell towers, altars featuring ornate engravings, and reliefs of angels and saints extending out of ceilings. Several of these churches stand in various cities around the state of Minas Gerais. Two examples are Our Lady of Mount Carmo Church and the São Francisco Chapel. These two churches represent the best of baroque art in Brazil and are considered among the world's finest. Both of them are found in the historical town of Ouro Prêto, which has been declared a World Cultural Monument by the United Nations.

Two blocks from the São Francisco Chapel is the town's monument to Aleijadinho, with his remains buried beneath a marker in a museum church. Some of his wood and soapstone carvings, documents about his career, and the illustrated Bibles he used to study are also displayed in the galleries of the church.

The town of Ouro Prêto is Brazil's monument to baroque art.

BRASÍLIA'S ARCHITECTURE

Brasília, a planned city built from scratch to be Brazil's capital, might some day be declared a World Cultural Monument.

Just as Aleijadinho became a driving force behind the baroque architecture of the town of Ouro Prêto, so another famous Brazilian architect is the mastermind of many of the modern ideas seen in the buildings of Brasília.

Oscar Niemeyer has designed numerous buildings in France, Algeria, the United States, and all over Brazil. In Brasília, he teamed up with noted city planner Lucio Costa and artist Roberto Burle-Marx to create his most famous works.

One word sums up Niemeyer's style: simplicity. Never curve a wall when a flat wall will do. Never use bright paints or bricks when the natural color of marble or concrete will be more effective.

Brasília's architecture

The three principal government buildings that border Brasília's Plaza of the Three Powers exhibit Niemeyer's practical design. The twin towers of the national congress dominate the square, with a concrete dome alongside one tower offsetting an inverted concrete dome next to the other.

The president's Planalto Palace and the Supreme Court flank the congress building. Both are similar in design. A long walkway leads up to a large patio, which surrounds a square structure with glass facades on all sides.

Eight pairs of identical government ministry buildings line an esplanade leading up to the Plaza of the Three Powers. The closest ministry to the Plaza, however, has its own unique design. Called the Itamarati Palace, the Foreign Ministry is a glass box encased in a concrete cage sitting in the middle of a pool of water.

The structures may look stark, but when the red evening sun reflects off the glass of the Planalto Palace or the waters around the Itamarati Palace, Brasília takes on a unique beauty.

The outline of Niemeyer's buildings against the bright sky of Brazil's Central Plateau reminds the people of the ultimate symbolism of this planned capital: an expression of their nation's desire to conquer its isolated interior regions.

Today, Niemeyer continues to be Brazil's premier architect. His most recent contribution is the famed Sambódromo, Rio's Carnival grandstand.

A statue honoring those who built Brasília.

LEISURE

BRAZILIANS LOVE SPORTS. There are 8,000 sports clubs all over the country. The long coastline encourages water sports such as surfing. Basketball and volleyball are played in all schools and clubs. Brazil has even won the World Basketball Championship twice. Tennis, boxing, and chess are also popular.

SOCCER IS KING

Brazilians joke that they save Sunday for two religious ceremonies: they go to church, and then they go to a soccer match.

No sport in Brazil rivals soccer in the sheer enthusiasm of its fans. Brazilian athletes have won medals in sports ranging from swimming to volleyball to track-and-field. But any time you see Brazilian children playing on an open patch of ground, odds are they will be kicking a soccer ball. Scoring a goal in the world's soccer championship is the dream of every Brazilian boy.

Brazilians call soccer *futebol* ("FOOT-ball"), the Portuguese spelling of the English word "football." Soccer came to Brazil from England about one hundred years ago. Most people would agree that Brazilians not only improved the game but perfected it.

The Brazilian style of play, with its superb dribbling, flamboyant showmanship, graceful playmaking, and incredible goals, has continued to delight the world. To Brazilians, the result of a match is not the only thing that matters; the way goals are scored is just as important. Time after time, Brazil seems to be able to pick superb players from out of nowhere and make them the envy of the world. Brazil is the only nation that has played in all 16 World Cup tournaments, and in 1994 it became the only country to win the competition four times.

SOCCER PASSION Soccer enthusiasts around the world consider Brazil's most famous star, Pelé, to be the greatest player of all time. A member of three of Brazil's world championship teams, Pelé scored more than 1,200 goals in national and international competitions. In Brazil's penultimate championship triumph during the 1970 World Cup in Mexico, Pelé combined with such legends as Tostao, Rivelino, Gerson, and Jairzinho to form a team most experts agree to be the greatest in history.

When Brazil's national team plays, the nation comes to a halt. Work stops, traffic disappears from the streets, even the beaches are deserted. Every television network broadcasts the match, along with several radio networks. Radio announcers break into the familiar extended cry of "gooooooooaaaaal" when Brazil scores. Fireworks erupt across the skies and people pour into the streets to celebrate victory.

A match between Santa Cruz and Flamengo in the Maracana Stadium. In 1950, the stadium seated 200,000 spectators for the deciding match of the World Cup. Brazil lost to Uruguay, plunging the nation into mourning.

On a smaller scale, this same enthusiasm accompanies matches played almost every day all over the country. There are countless leagues for children, teenagers, and adults. Besides the regular game played on a grass field with 11 players to each side, Brazilians also play beach soccer on the sand with seven players to each side, and indoor soccer on a hard surface with six players to each side. There is even a league that plays "car soccer." The players drive cars on an oversized field, pushing a huge balloon-like ball around.

THE FLA-FLU RIVALRY Rivalries are common in Brazilian soccer, but few rivalries in the world can match the intensity of clashes between Rio de Janeiro's super clubs, Flamengo and Fluminense. Brazilians refer to these matches as "Fla-Flu."

Fans assemble throughout the city the morning of the game. Dressed in their teams' colors and carrying team flags, they dance and sing from the moment they gather. As the afternoon progresses, thousands of chanting supporters converge on Rio's mammoth Maracana Stadium, which has a capacity of 200,000. The red and black shirts of Flamengo fans color one side of the stadium, while the red, white, and green of Fluminense dominate the other.

By the time the teams take to the field in the late afternoon, the samba beat has already whipped the fans into a frenzy. They greet the players with an explosion of fireworks and a sea of waving flags. Flamengo fans throw confetti, while Fluminense supporters heave talcum powder into the air. All eyes are focused on the field when the game begins. Like a wave, noise rises and falls from one end of the stadium to the other, as the teams take turns dictating the play. The wave of noise crests when a goal is scored. Players on the field and fans in the stands leap into the air and exchange hugs. The flags and fireworks reappear.

At the end of the game, the losing team's supporters fold up their flags, put away their drumsticks, and head home in sorrow. The winners take their party to the streets, hang their flags out of windows, honk car horns, and keep the samba beat going throughout the night. Radio stations will replay narratives of the goals. Monday newspapers will offer diagrams depicting how each goal was scored, along with commentaries on the performance of each player, coach, and referee. Talk of the game goes on everywhere, until the next Sunday's feature match.

One of the "must see" attractions when visiting Brazil is a soccer match. Brazilian soccer fans are known to be some of the most fanatical and enthusiastic in the world. Organized groups of supporters wave banners and can break out into song and dance with unbridled fervor at any time during the match. Even if the game gets boring, fan-watching is itself a real treat.

103

BEACH FUN

Most people in Brazil live a short bus ride from the ocean, and the beach is a part of daily life.

Brazilians take great pride in the fact that their beaches are open to all—in many places, the law prohibits private ownership of any part of the beach. Some sociologists even attribute the relative lack of tension between Brazil's social classes to the "democracy" of the beach. When a man is on the beach in his bathing suit, you do not know if he is upper- or lower-class. The conclusion is that as long as the poor can mingle freely with the wealthy on the beach, they do not feel oppressed.

In practice, however, groups with different interests congregate on their own stretch of the beach, informally dividing the sand into little communities. On any beach in Rio de Janeiro, artists and intellectuals frequent one area, members of a political party regularly meet in another. Families with small children stay in one place, teenagers hang around another. The best surfers convene on one stretch, the best volleyball games are found elsewhere. The regulars on the different patches of beach get to know one another. Making a trip to the beach is an opportunity to catch up with the latest news and gossip.

Early in the morning, people go to the beaches to exercise. Lifeguards lead group calisthenic sessions, but the favorite form of exercise is the Cooper Test, a 2.5-mile (4-km) run named after an American doctor who was one of the early advocates of jogging. Signs along the beaches in many cities mark out the distances, and runners crowd the sidewalks in the early morning and late afternoon.

Above: **Rio de Janeiro's famed Ipanema—"Dangerous Waters"—beach. The Ipanema neighborhood, Rio's style and culture center, boasts one of the most expensive stretches of real estate in the world.**

Opposite: **A carnival on a beach in Salvador.**

105

A VIEW FROM THE SAND

When the sun gets higher in the sky, sunbathers begin to arrive. During the week, many Brazilians take a quick trip to the beach during lunch breaks.

On a sunny weekend, Brazilians cram the beaches by the thousands. Most of them lie on the sand and relax, but it is hardly a quiet atmosphere. Vendors march up and down selling sweets, fruit juices, hot coffee, a local brand of tea called *mate,* soft drinks, ice cream, hot dogs, and an impressive array of beach knickknacks.

A beach vendor selling hats and suntan oil.

Games are played everywhere. Soccer and volleyball boundaries are marked off, complete with makeshift goalposts and nets. Children fly bird-shaped kites. Other beach-goers hit rubber balls back and forth using paddles or swat a *peteca* ("pay-TAY-kah"), a device consisting of long feathers weighted by a bundle of sand wrapped in leather, with their hands.

Before going home, beach-goers stop at one of the open-air cafés along the beach for a drink or a quick bite.

Gradually, the afternoon crowd gives way to the night crowd. Couples stroll along the sand holding hands. The boardwalk in many cities becomes an outdoor arts fair, with artisans selling goods from paintings to woven hammocks. Music and conversation continue in the open-air cafés until late at night.

DANCE MUSIC

While for most of the year, samba never strays far from their thoughts, during Carnival, samba is all Brazilians have on their mind. Any time a group of Brazilians get together, be it on the beach, in a bus, at a restaurant, or in a soccer stadium, if there is a can to tap or a box of matches to shake, a samba beat is likely to start.

A group of Brazilian researchers in the Antarctica said that they survived the unfamiliar freezing temperatures by warming up with a daily improvised samba session.

When they are not making their own music, Brazilians love to dance to music played by others. Even in small farming communities of the southern and northeastern interior, you can count on finding somewhere to dance any night.

Capoeira dancers perform on Ipanema Beach. *Capoeira* is a martial arts dance first introduced by the slaves. Told by their masters to stop, the slaves disguised this foot-fighting technique as a dance, thereby preserving the cultural art form.

MUSIC FEVER

In a major city like Rio de Janeiro, the choice for samba is staggering. The large samba schools raise money and practice for the annual Carnival parade by holding samba parties at their headquarters all year round. These performances draw huge crowds, but smaller bands play samba music in a cozier atmosphere in many nightclubs around town.

String bands playing *choro* music cannot match the samba beat, but still provide lively dance music. Another option is the *gafieira* ("gah-fee-AY-rah"), a dance hall where Brazilian-style ballroom dancing is practiced. The *maxixe* ("mah-SHIH-shih"), a favorite dance, combines the rapid rhythms of African and Latin music with the steps of a European polka. Watching the couples swirl around the floor can make spectators dizzy.

Some clubs feature *frevo* ("FRAY-voh") dancing, a style Brazilians in the northeast prefer over samba during Carnival. Lovers of music from the northeast can choose other night spots where *forró* ("FOH-hoh") bands perform. The accordion is the main instrument for this kind of music, the favorite of the *sertão* region. Urban Brazilians sometimes joke about *forró* music, much the way some Americans joke about hillbilly music.

As if homegrown music is not enough, Brazilians also love imported music. Dance and music enthusiasts pack discos, rock-and-roll halls, and jazz clubs. One of the biggest crowds in the history of Rio de Janeiro's giant soccer stadium came to see a Frank Sinatra concert.

An afternoon rock concert.

TELEVISION SOAPS

Television has joined music, soccer, and the beach as a cornerstone of Brazilian leisure activity. TV Globo, Brazil's largest network, is the fourth largest in the world. Only the three principal U.S. networks operate more stations. Four smaller networks also operate in Brazil.

Most of the shows on the air are made in Brazil. The most popular are the *telenovelas* ("teh-leh-noh-VEH-lahs"), long-running serials aired during prime time. These programs can be watched every night, but TV Globo's feature show, the one bringing together the most stars and the best production team, comes on the air every week night at 8:30 P.M. Just as life stops for soccer games on Sundays, many Brazilians refuse to schedule anything during the week at this time.

A survey conducted in Brazil suggests that about 80 percent of television viewers tune in to local prime time shows called *novela* ("noh-VEH-la"). These programs are extremely influential; they introduce new slang and expressions into Brazilian discourse and new trends into Brazilian fashion.

Although they portray Brazilian characters in Brazilian settings, TV Globo's serials have become hits all over the world. They have been dubbed, for example, in Italian for viewers in Italy and even in Chinese for countries with a large Chinese-speaking viewership.

If you do not own a television set, you can always catch the latest soap opera at the electronics store.

FESTIVALS

É CARNAVAL! IT'S CARNIVAL TIME! Every year, this cry fills the air to start a four-day national holiday. Everyone forgets his or her problems, puts on a costume, and dances to the rhythms of samba, *frevo,* and *lambada* ("lahm-BAH-deh") music.

Brazilians adore music, dancing, and partying. Festive parties are a part of many religious festivals, but the biggest party of all is Carnival. Dating back to early Christian times, this event began as a last chance to feast before the beginning of Lent. While Carnival is celebrated in countries around the world, no other country's celebration matches the frenzy and excitement of Carnival in Brazil.

Carnival takes place some time in late February to early March. Traditionally, it starts the Sunday before Lent and ends on Ash Wednesday, but Brazilians extend the party to a week. During this period, mayors ceremonially hand over the keys of their cities to King Momo, an ancient Greek god of mockery and jest. Streets are closed to traffic, and thousands throng streets and beaches to sing, dance, and cheer the parades in Brazil's biggest, most colorful party.

Opposite and below: **Carnival is deeply rooted in ethnic and religious heritage. Some say the word** *carnival* **comes from the Italian** *Carne Vale,* **which means "farewell to meat," since it marks the last days before Lent. Others say it is derived from the Latin** *Carrum Novalis,* **the Roman festival float.**

CARNIVAL IN RIO DE JANEIRO

The most famous festivities take place in Rio de Janeiro. The biggest event is the parade of the 26 best *escolas de samba* ("ess-KOH-lahs deh SAHM-bah"), or samba schools, along the Sambódromo, a street lined with grandstands. For three nights, thousands watch the elaborately dressed participants dance and sing their way down the parade route.

On Ash Wednesday, an official jury announces its choice for the best school in that year's parade, and the winner's celebration extends the Carnival joy through the weekend.

Dancing is not restricted to the Sambódromo. Merrymakers called *foliões* ("foh-lee-OH-ehs") take over the city streets, dressed in clown outfits or swimwear. Groups wearing the same costumes make up a *bloco*

("BLOH-koh"). The best known is the *Bloco das Piranhas*, a group of men who take to the streets dressed as women. The *blocos* and *foliões* fall in behind various small samba bands that roam on foot or by car, and spontaneous street parties may erupt anywhere.

Private clubs throw extravagant parties attended by as many as 10,000 people. The most famous is the "Night in Baghdad" theme ball on the last night of Carnival. Party-goers wear either a tuxedo or a costume. In the heat of the crammed ballroom, most opt for the latter.

Samba music and dancing keep the temperature high from midnight until well past breakfast the next morning.

Samba dancers parade along the Sambódromo with baskets of flowers and fruit. Dancers train the whole year for Carnival, which lasts only a few days.

CARNIVAL IN SALVADOR AND RECIFE

Less vibrant *escola de samba* parades take place in other cities, but the favorite Carnival spots after Rio are in the northeast. The street celebrations in Salvador da Bahia and Recife are almost as intense as Rio's.

Frevo music replaces the samba as the favorite. Based on African rhythms, it originated in Recife. Today, the city's expert *frevo* dancers perform in traditional fashion, wearing knee-length pants, long stockings, and baggy shirts, and waving bright umbrellas.

Children dressed as clowns take to the streets for a party.

An African dance in Salvador.

The trademark of Salvador's Carnival is a specially equipped truck called the *trio eletrico*. Loudspeakers lining the sides of this truck blast music played by a band on top. The crowds following the truck dance to various types of music, from the traditional *frevo* to the more recent *deboche* ("deh-BOHSH") or *lambada*. These newer rhythms draw upon samba, *frevo,* and outside influences such as reggae and rock-and-roll.

Afoxés ("ah-foh-SHEH") also march through the streets of Salvador. Made up of followers of African religions, they sprinkle lavender cologne on the crowd and sing sacred songs, often in African languages.

Recife has neither samba schools nor *trio eletricos,* but there is no shortage of *frevo* bands and costumed *blocos* along its streets. It also has its *maracatu* ("mah-rah-kah-TOO") marches, the royal procession of African kings. First practiced by slaves longing for their homeland, the *maracatu* is today reenacted by African groups in Brazil. Other groups wear feathered headdresses and paint their faces to perform the *caboclinho* ("kah-boh-KLEE-oh"), a frenetic dance learned from the Indians.

ESCOLAS DE SAMBA

It's Carnival, and one of Rio's best *escolas de samba* has filled the mile-long (1.6-km-long) Sambódromo. The school's 3,000 dancers sing and swing to a samba beat pounded out by a 250-member percussion section. Gigantic floats separate groups of dancers dressed in bright costumes. For an hour and a half, this wave of color and sound makes its way along the avenue. The samba schools take turns parading before the huge crowds. Starting at around 8 P.M., they go on until at least nine o'clock the next morning.

The schools are actually neighborhood associations, most coming from the poorer areas of the city. All year long, members volunteer their time to put together the extravagant costumes and floats and practice their song and dance routines. Each school's presentation is built around a theme song called *samba enredo*. Through the floats and costumes, they build their theme into a story.

Generally, the theme is Brazilian folklore or history. Occasionally, it makes a humorous comment on modern life. In 1990, a group took a theme revolving around a Rio de Janeiro neighborhood known for its sale of stolen property. The percussion section wore police uniforms while some of the costumes and floats portrayed jails, weapons, car tires, and television sets.

The structure of each parade follows a set formula. First comes the *abre alas*, or opening wing. Accompanied by the first float, this group introduces the main theme. A line of men in dark suits follows. They are the school's figurative board of directors, intended to add an air of dignity to the fun.

The samba starts in earnest with the arrival of the *mestre sala* and *porta bandeira*, the school's dance master and flag bearer respectively. The different wings follow, separated by floats and groups of *passistos* ("pah-SEES-toos"), the school's most skilled samba dancers, performing elaborate dance steps and acrobatic leaps.

Each school also features a *baiana* wing, in which Afro-Brazilian women in traditional clothing celebrate the African origin of the Brazilian samba. The percussion section, called the *bateria* ("bah-teh-REE-ah"), starts near the front but pulls up along the avenue for the last group of dancers to catch up so that they can keep up with the beat.

NATIONAL HOLIDAYS

January 1	New Year's Day
February/March	Carnival (four days)
March/April	Good Friday and Easter Sunday
April 21	Tiradentes Day (honoring a famous Brazilian patriot)
May 1	Labor Day
May/June	Corpus Christi
September 7	Independence Day
October 12	Our Lady of Aparecida (patron saint of Brazil)
November 2	All Souls' Day
November 15	Proclamation of the Republic
December 25	Christmas

OKTOBERFEST

The biggest festival in the south of Brazil has nothing to do with Africa or the Catholic Church. The Oktoberfest in Blumenau, Santa Catarina, started only in 1982, is now the world's second largest beer festival. In 1988, over a million people drank 200,000 gallons (757,082 liters) of beer during the 16-day event. Only the original Oktoberfest in Munich, Germany, exceeds this scale. German immigrants founded Blumenau, and during October, there is little evidence of the New World in the city. People listening to the polka bands, eating *wurst* with sauerkraut, or watching the blonde, blue-eyed women serving beer in the *biergarten* would be convinced they were in Germany.

RELIGIOUS FESTIVALS

Catholic holy days make up about half of Brazil's national holidays. The feast day of Brazil's patron saint, Nossa Senhora de Aparecida, is unique. In 1717, fishermen in the state of São Paulo found a statue of the Virgin Mary in a river. They built a chapel, and a cult grew around the statue. Today, the chapel has become a huge basilica, sitting along the Rio–São Paulo highway. About eight million devotees visit the church each year, over a million during the month of October.

Nativity sets and Santa Claus are both a part of Christmas in Brazil. Instead of arriving through the chimney, children believe that *Papai Noel* comes in through the window and leaves presents in shoes left on the floor. More important than the gift-giving is the traditional Christmas Eve dinner, which brings together the entire extended family.

Numerous other religious days are observed across the country. The feast days of saints Anthony (June 12), John (June 23), and Peter (June 28) fall close enough to one another to justify two weeks of partying, called *festas juninas* ("FEHS-tahs joo-NEE-nahs"). People dress in country style to attend outdoor parties featuring Brazilian country music and cooking. Fireworks, bonfires, and religious processions are other elements of the festivities. Saint Anthony is the patron saint of single men and women, so staged wedding ceremonies are often played out on his feast day.

Many religious festivals are unique to different regions. New Year's Eve in Rio de Janeiro is the feast day of Iemanja, the African goddess of rivers and water. At midnight, her followers flock to the beach to launch gifts on

A merry musician puts on a bright smile, depicting the attitude of Brazilians when they celebrate the nation's many festivals.

tiny boats. Tradition says that the goddess will not accept the gifts of those without virtue, so their boats will wash back to shore. To prevent this from happening, believers wade as far out from the beach as possible before releasing their offerings.

The same ceremony takes place in Salvador on February 2. On New Year's Day, Salvador joins other northeastern towns in celebrating the feast of the Lord Jesus of the Navigators. A parade of colorfully decorated ships escorts a statue of Jesus Christ across the harbor, as sailors believe that their homage to the Lord will protect them from harm.

FOOD

BRAZIL'S CUISINE MIRRORS ITS CULTURE. Brazilians use methods and ingredients introduced by European immigrants and African slaves in the past and by indigenous Indians past and present. As with culture, the degree of influence of each contributor varies according to region.

The two staples of the Brazilian diet are manioc flour and beans. Manioc comes from the cassava plant. Indians on the northeastern coast cultivated this plant when the Portuguese first arrived in Brazil.

The Portuguese brought beans with them, as well as rice, sugarcane, and coffee. Traders on their way back from the Far East delivered cloves, cinnamon, and other spices. African slaves introduced bananas and a type of palm oil called *dendê* ("dehn-DAY"). *Dendê* oil remains a key ingredient in the typical dishes of the northeast.

Opposite: **A vegetable market on a street in historic Ouro Prêto.**

Left: **A fisherman's family comes together to have a meal.**

FEIJOADA

Despite regional differences, there is one dish that brings the country together. The *feijoada* ("fay-jhoo-AH-dah") is a weekly ritual in many restaurants and homes. The classic *feijoada* served in Rio de Janeiro combines black beans and various types of dried and smoked meats. This meal has developed with help from all three of Brazil's ethnic roots. Along with rice, a fried manioc-flour dish called *farofa* ("fah-ROH-fah") is the main complement of the *feijoada*.

The original *feijoada* recipe came from African slaves. In colonial days, the master kept the best cuts of meat for his family, giving his slaves the unwanted parts like the feet of the pig or the tongue of the cow. The slaves threw these leftovers into a pot with their beans, added onions, garlic, and a few other spices, and created a dish that eventually caught the master's attention.

The simple *feijoada,* in all its elegance. The humble bean recipe has been crowned Brazil's national dish.

Today, many restaurants in Brazil serve two types of *feijoada*: *feijoada tipica* ("TEE-pih-kah") contains the traditional ingredients, including the eyes, ears, tongue, and tail of the animal; *feijoada moderna* ("moh-DEHR-nah") sticks to more conventional cuts such as pork loin and beef brisket. Prepared either way, the end result is a delicious meal over which Brazilians can linger for two to three hours.

People warm up with a *caiprinha* ("kah-ee-pee-REEN-yah"), an alcoholic drink made with lime, sugar, and *cachaça* ("kah-SHAH-sah"), which is a liquor distilled from sugarcane. The main meal follows: a helping or two of the beans, meat, rice, *farofa*, fresh oranges, and fried chopped kale.

BAHIAN FOOD

Bahia is home to Brazil's most distinctive cuisine. In this state, Portuguese and African styles of cooking combined with seafood and the tropical food of the northeastern coast produce a unique cuisine.

A *baiana* sells—and samples—her products in an open-air market.

To foreigners, Bahian food does not always look appetizing. Its ingredients are usually mashed and mixed in one pot and served over rice, manioc, or cornmeal. But the rich taste of the ingredients, including *dendê* oil, coconut milk, dried shrimp or fish, crabmeat, and cashew nuts, soon wins over those who try it. The piquant taste of *malagueta* ("mah-lah-GAY-tah") chili peppers balances the richness of these flavors. For those who like their food extra spicy, a bowl of pepper usually accompanies a Bahian dish.

Baianas are considered Brazil's best bakers of sweet food, though they are also famous for their main dishes. Dressed in white, *baianas* sell their specialties along the streets of cities like Salvador. Local favorites include *moqueca* ("moh-EH-kah"), *vatapá* ("vah-tah-PAH"), *caruru* ("kah-ROO-roo"), and *acarajé* ("ah-kah-rah-JEH"). *Moqueca* is a stew based on *dendê* oil, coconut milk, fish, or shrimp and spiced by *malagueta* peppers, garlic, and cloves. *Vatapá* is also a stew with ingredients similar to those in *moqueca*, except that it is thicker because manioc flour is added, and it tastes a little different because ginger is used in place of cloves. *Caruru* is a dish of shrimp and okra boiled in water, spiced with onions and peppers, and then mixed with *dendê* oil. *Acarajé* is a Brazilian fast food, the rough equivalent of the American hamburger. It is made from soaked and skinned local *fradinho* ("frah-JIN-uh") beans, which are mashed together, mixed with diced shrimp and onions, and then fried in *dendê* oil.

PREPARING MANIOC FLOUR

Farmers in the north and northeast still prepare manioc flour from the roots of the cassava plant, using the same technique indigenous Indians have been using for 400 years, although modern farmers employ slightly more advanced technologies.

After the roots of the cassava plant have been picked and peeled, they are chopped in a grinder called a *cevadeira* ("say-vah-DAY-reh"). Metal blades inside this grinder are spun by a turning wheel.

Yanomami Indians grate manioc flour to make soup for 100 guests.

The roots of the cassava plant contain poisonous prussic acid. To extract this poison, farmers use a levered press to pound the chopped cassava. The liquid that runs off contains the acid, and a paste that is left behind is what is wanted. This paste is run through a sieve to separate the thicker part, called *crueira* ("croo-EH-rah").

The thin paste is boiled in an open pot and stirred constantly until it has been roasted dry. This powder is manioc flour.

PAPOS DE ANJO (ANGEL'S CHEEKS)

These are sweet babas (small yeast cakes). Called "angel's cheeks," they may have been invented by nuns.

2 egg whites	2 ¹/₂ cups (590 ml) superfine sugar
6 egg yolks	2 cups (470 ml) water
1 teaspoon yeast	1 teaspoon vanilla extract
1 teaspoon flour	
4 tablespoons butter	

1. Beat the egg whites until stiff. Add the egg yolks one at a time, beating continuously.
2. Add the yeast and flour. Beat until a thick cream forms.
3. Grease 20 small muffin tins. Fill them ³/₄ full with the mixture.
4. Place tins in the oven at 400°F (204°C) and bake for 20 minutes.
5. Remove the baked cakes from the tins and arrange them on a shallow tray.
6. Mix the sugar, water, and vanilla extract to make a syrup.
7. Pour the syrup over the *papos de anjo*, allowing the syrup to soak into the cakes. Turn the cakes over so that they are evenly soaked.

An Indian fisherman shoots for fish with his bow and arrow at the Xingu National Park.

OTHER REGIONAL FOODS

Seafood is the favorite food in most of the north. *Sururu* ("soo-roo-ROO"), a clam stew prepared in oyster sauce, and stuffed crab are favorite dishes in the state of Pernambuco. *Pirão* ("pee-RAH-oo"), a porridge prepared with manioc and fish broth, often accompanies seafood.

Fresh meat and fish can be hard to come by in the hot northeastern *sertão*. *Carne de sol* ("KAH-neh deh SOH"), or dried salted meat, has become a staple. After slaughtering a cow, ranchers rub salt into the meat and hang it on racks to dry in the sun and wind. Another favorite in the *sertão* is the *buchada* ("boo-SHAH-dah"), a dish made from goat's liver, heart, and tripe.

The influence of indigenous Indians is still strong in the north as the names of many dishes reveal. Residents of the states of Pará and Amazonas often eat fresh *pirarucu* ("pee-rah-roo-KOO") and *tucunare* ("too-koo-nah-REH") fish served with a manioc sauce called *tucupi* ("too-koo-PEE"). They also enjoy a number of fruits unique to the Amazon. In the south, *churrasco* ("shoo-HAHS-koo"), meat on a spit slowly grilled and basted with saltwater for flavor, is the most popular meal. Brazilians either cook *churrascos* at home or go to *churrascaria* ("shoo-hahs-kah-REE-ah") restaurants, where they eat all they can for a fixed price.

FRUITS OF BRAZIL

The forests of Brazil are a treasure chest of exquisite fruits. Ice-cream shops in cities like Belém in Pará advertise 99 exotic fruit flavors. But a U.S. or European visitor would have a hard time identifying most of these flavors. Here are a few examples of the fruits of Brazil:

AÇAÍ ("ah-sah-EE") is the fruit of a palm tree called the *açaizeiro* ("ah-sah-ee-ZAY-roh"). It is common in the states of Amazonas and Pará. The flesh is usually mixed with sugar and served in a gourd or else used to make wine. Northerners insist that any visitor who drinks *açai* wine will visit the region again.

GRAVIOLA ("grah-vee-OH-lah") comes from the same family as the pineapple. It is an oval-shaped fruit weighing one to two pounds (0.5 to 0.9 kg). A white, creamy meat and fine dark seeds lie inside its pale green skin. It tastes like a cross between a banana and a pineapple.

JABUTICABA ("jah-boo-chih-KAH-beh") is a red or black berry that originally grew in the wild, but is now cultivated in different parts of Brazil. Its sweet, white pulp is used to make pies, jellies, or wine.

JACA ("JAAH-kah") is the jackfruit from Southeast Asia. Traders brought it to Brazil in the 18th century, and it thrives in the tropical climate. The fruit can weigh up to 40 pounds (18 kg), but its pulp tastes rather sour. Brazilians use the pulp to make sweets or jellies and eat the seeds roasted.

GOIABA ("goh-YAH-bah"), or guava, is a yellow, pear-shaped fruit grown all over Brazil. One of the favorite fruits in the country, it is believed to stimulate the appetite when eaten before a meal and to aid digestion when eaten afterward.

JENIPAPO ("jeh-nih-PAH-poo") is a light-brown fruit about the size of an apple. It originated in the Antilles and thrives in Brazil's north, where Indians use its dark pulp to blacken their faces. When ripe, the *jenipapo* skin is thin and soft, and the watery pulp has a sweet and sour taste.

CUSTOMS

Breakfast is usually a light meal for most Brazilians, with some fruit accompanying buttered bread and coffee. Lunch, generally the biggest meal of the day, regularly takes up to two hours. Many employers grant extended lunch breaks to allow workers to enjoy this meal at home. Dinner is served quite late, usually around 8:30 P.M. In between lunch and dinner, many people have a *lanche* ("LAHN-cheh"), a light snack with coffee or juice.

Like good grammar, Brazilians consider good table manners to be a sign of a good education and hence of good social standing. Those with good manners do not use bare hands to pick up food. They use a fork and knife for everything, including apples, oranges, sandwiches, chicken legs, and pizzas. A growing number of U.S.-style fast-food restaurants are gradually changing this rule, but many people carefully wrap a napkin around their hamburgers.

A Brazilian family gathers to eat, while junior cries at the far end of the table.

Children may eat an ice-cream cone while walking down the street, but Brazilians consider it rude for an adult to eat in public. Those who buy food from a streetside vendor usually eat it on the spot. This habit stems from the belief that food should be shared. Any time Brazilians are eating, whether it be a meal at home or a candy bar on the beach, they offer to share it with any friend who comes along.

When food is offered, it is considered rude to say no without offering a good excuse. Similarly, hosts are expected to provide more than enough food for their guests, and guests are expected to try their best to eat all of it.

DRINKS

Coffee is Brazil's national drink. A *cafezinho* ("kah-feh-ZEEN-yoo") is a mandatory part of any social event, be it lunch with the family at home or a business meeting in the office. *Cafezinho* means "little coffee," and this very strong brew is served in a cup one-third the size of an American coffee cup.

Brazilians add lots of sugar to their *cafezinho* to counter the strength of the brew. Businesspeople in Brazil always start their meetings with *cafezinhos* all round. They

A popular *cafezinho* bar.

have a friendly chat while drinking, and serious talk begins only when the cups are empty. The opposite occurs at mealtime; the *cafezinho* comes after the meal is finished.

Good drink and conversation are trademarks of the sidewalk bars and cafés. Whether stopping by on the way home from the beach or meeting friends after dinner, Brazilians spend a lot of time in bars and cafés. They drink fruit juices, such as coconut milk or freshly squeezed mango, and fruit milkshakes.

Popular milkshakes use ingredients such as raw oatmeal, avocado, papaya, and banana. *Guarana* ("goo-ah-rah-NAH"), a unique Brazilian soft drink, is made from a small tropical fruit. Beer and *cachaça* are popular at night. Bartenders combine *cachaça* with different fruits to make drinks called *batidas* ("bah-CHEE-dahs").

Wine is becoming increasingly popular. Almost all of Brazil's wine comes from Rio Grande do Sul, where vineyards started by Italian immigrants continue to improve the quality of Brazilian wine.

FEIJOADA

This is Brazil's national dish. *Feijoa* means "black beans" in Protuguese. This recipe serves 5.

1 pound (455 g) black beans
10 cups (2.5 liters) water
2 cups (470 ml) beef stock
1 pound (455 g) smoked sausage
½ pound (228 g) bacon
4 pork shoulder bones and ears

3 tablespoons olive oil
2 small onions
2 garlic cloves
2 large bay leaves
Salt and fresh pepper
Hot pepper sauce

Wash black beans well and soak in 4 cups (1 liter) water overnight. Add beef stock and cook for an hour over low heat, stirring occasionally to avoid burning. Cut sausage, bacon, and pork into bite-size pieces and place in a pan. Cover with 5 cups (1.2 liters) water and boil for 10 minutes, then carefully drain away water. Heat olive oil in a pan and fry onions and garlic to form a caramel. Add some of the cooked beans to the fried onions and garlic and mash. Add bay leaves and fry for a few minutes. Pour mixture into the rest of the cooked beans. Add the strained meats and 1 cup (235 ml) water. Stir, then add salt and hot pepper sauce to taste. When the liquid is thick and flavorful, serve over rice and garnish with orange slices.

RABANADAS (PORTUGUESE FRIED TOAST)

This recipe serves 4 to 6 people.

8 slices white bread
2 cups (470 ml) milk
2 tablespoons plus 1 cup (235 ml) sugar
1 tablespoon ground cinnamon

Pinch of salt
3 large eggs, separated
1 cup (235 ml) vegetable oil

Heat oven on low setting. Cut bread in half diagonally, or use a cookie cutter to cut out circles. Put milk and 2 tablespoons of sugar in a large, shallow bowl and stir. Leave bread to soak in milk and sugar mixture for 10 minutes. Mix cinnamon, salt, and the rest of the sugar together in a bowl. Set aside. Put egg whites in a clean bowl. Using an electric mixer, beat until egg whites are thick and stand in stiff peaks when the beaters are lifted. Add egg yolks and beat again until thick. Heat a few tablespoons of oil in a large skillet over medium heat. Remove bread from milk, slice by slice, and dip in eggs. Add

to skillet and fry until golden. Using a spatula, turn over. Continue frying until golden. Drain on paper towels. Put on a plate and sprinkle cinnamon sugar. Keep warm in oven.

PÉ-DE-MOLEQUE

This is a peanut snack.

3 cups (710 ml) sugar
1 ½ cups (355 ml) water
1 cup (235 ml) light corn syrup

3 egg yolks, beaten
2 cups (470 ml) coarsely chopped
   roasted peanuts

Lightly grease a shallow baking pan. Leave aside. Put sugar in a pot over low heat. Add water and stir until sugar dissolves. Stir in corn syrup. Turn up heat and boil until mixture reaches 250–265°F (120–130°C). Carefully stir in egg yolks. Using a fork, twirl yolks to make "threads." Stir in peanuts. Carefully pour mixture into baking pan. Using a greased knife, mark squares in the mixture, but do not cut. Leave to cool and set. To serve, cut into squares.

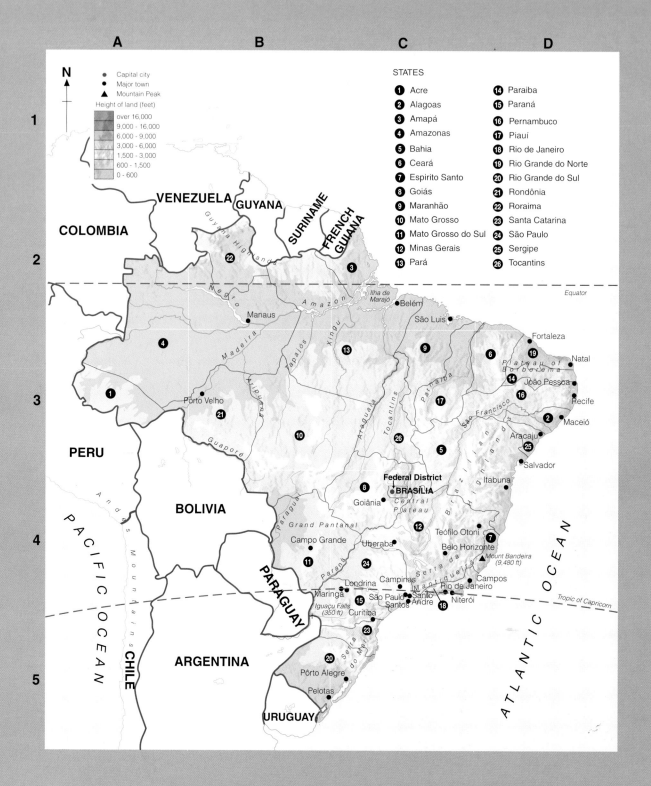

MAP OF BRAZIL

ECONOMIC BRAZIL

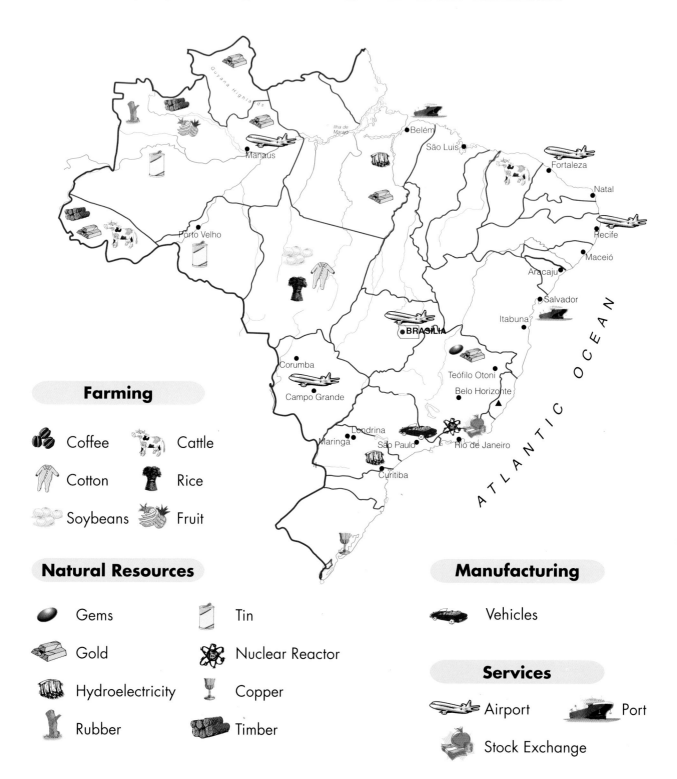

Farming

🫘 Coffee   🐄 Cattle

👕 Cotton   🌳 Rice

☁️ Soybeans   🍇 Fruit

Natural Resources

Gems   Tin

Gold   Nuclear Reactor

Hydroelectricity   Copper

Rubber   Timber

Manufacturing

Vehicles

Services

Airport   Port

Stock Exchange

ABOUT
THE ECONOMY

INDUSTRIES
Textiles, shoes, chemicals, cement, lumber, iron ore, tin, steel, aircraft, motor vehicles and parts, other machinery, and equipment

GROSS DOMESTIC PRODUCT (GDP)
US$1.057 trillion (1999)

GDP PER CAPITA
US$6,150 (1999)

GDP COMPOSITION
Agriculture: 14 percent
Industry: 36 percent
Services: 50 percent (1997)

GDP GROWTH
0.8 percent (1999)

EXTERNAL DEBT
$200 billion (1999)

INFLATION RATE
5 percent (1999)

CURRENCY
Real (R) = 100 centavos
US$1 = R$1.804

TOURIST ARRIVALS
2.85 million (1997)

AGRICULTURAL PRODUCTS
Coffee, soybeans, wheat, rice, corn, sugarcane, cocoa, citrus fruit, and beef

MAIN EXPORTS
Iron ore, soybean bran, wheat, rice, corn, sugarcane, cocoa, citrus fruit, and beef

MAIN EXPORT PARTNERS
United States 18 percent, Argentina 13 percent, Germany 5 percent, Netherlands 5 percent, and Japan 4 percent (1999)

MAIN IMPORTS
Crude oil, capital goods, chemicals, food, and coal

MAIN IMPORT PARTNERS
United States 23 percent, Argentina 12 percent, Germany 10 percent, Japan 5 percent, and Italy 5 percent (1999)

LABOR FORCE
74 million (1997 est.)

LABOR FORCE BY OCCUPATION
Services 42 percent, agriculture 31 percent, and industry 27 percent

UNEMPLOYMENT RATE
7.5 percent (1999)

CULTURAL BRAZIL

Amazonian Rain Forest
The lungs of the earth, this forest is home to many unique species of plant and animal, some of which are in danger of extinction, while others have yet to be discovered.

Feast of Our Lady of Nazareth
Some 2 million people participate in *Cirio*, a procession of faith in honor of Our Lady of Nazareth.

Folklore Festival
Characters from Brazilian folklore come to life through skits, music, and the clothing of Maracatu and Chula dancers.

Carnival
Crowds throng the streeets in a celebration of indulgences before 40 days of fasting and abstinence leading up to Easter.

Manaus Opera House
Also known as the Amazon Theater. Has a golden dome covered with 36,000 ceramic tiles, a ceiling painted with scenes of music, dance, and drama, and a seating capacity of 640.

Basílica do Senhor Bom Jesus de Matosinhos
Chapels here contain 64 life-size statues dramatizing the scenes of the Passion of Jesus Christ and 12 soapstone statues of Old Testament prophets.

Masquerades
Dancers, drummers, and singers dressed in elaborate costumes lead a massive, night-long street party filled with music, food, and alcohol.

Cristo Redentor
From the top of Corcovado (Hunchback) Mountain, a concrete statue of Christ the Redeemer—at a height of 125 feet (38 m) and spanning 92 feet (28 m) across the arms—towers over Rio de Janeiro.

Copacabana and Ipanema
World-famous beaches, one of the loveliest bays in the world, and a wonderful climate blending summer and springtime make Rio a true sun, sand, and sea city.

Iguaçu Falls
Some 275 waterfalls spread over a two-mile (3.2-km) area. The most spectacular point is at Devil's Throat, where 14 falls curve around a 269-foot (82-m) drop.

Oktoberfest
The second largest festival in Brazil and second largest beer festival in the world displays typical German dances and costumes to revive the customs and culture of German immigrants who came to Brazil.

Manaus

Belém

Recife

BRASÍLIA

Belo Horizonte

São Paulo

Rio de Janeiro

Iguaçu Falls
(350 ft)   Curitiba

Blumenau

ABOUT
THE CULTURE

OFFICIAL NAME
Federative Republic of Brazil

FLAG DESCRIPTION
Green background with a large yellow diamond in the center bearing a blue celestial globe with 27 white five-pointed stars arranged in the pattern of the night sky. The globe has a white equatorial band with the motto *Ordem E Progresso* ("Order and Progress").

POPULATION
172,860,370

LIFE EXPECTANCY
Total population 62.94 years
Male 58.54 years; female 67.56 years (2000 est.)

AGE STRUCTURE
0-14 years: 29 percent of population
15-64 years: 66 percent
65 years and over: 5 percent

ETHNIC GROUPS
Caucasian (Portuguese, German, Italian, Spanish, Polish) 55 percent, mixed Caucasian and African 38 percent, African 6 percent, others (Japanese, Arab, Amerindian) 1 percent

MAIN RELIGION
Roman Catholicism (90 percent of population)

MAJOR LANGUAGES
Portuguese (official), Spanish, English, French

LITERACY
83.3 percent of population aged 15 and above

ADMINISTRATIVE DIVISIONS
26 states (*estado*) and 1 federal district (*distrito federal*)

INDEPENDENCE DAY
September 7, 1822

NATIONAL HOLIDAY
New Year's Day (January 1), Carnival (February/March), Easter (March/April), Tirandentes Day (April 21), Labor Day (May 1), Corpus Christi (May/June), Independence Day (September 7), Our Lady of Aparecida (October 12), All Souls' Day (November 2), Proclamation of the Republc (November 15), Christmas (December 25)

CONSTITUTION
October 5, 1988

CHIEF OF STATE AND HEAD OF GOVERNMENT
President Fernando Henrique CARDOSO

SUFFRAGE
Voluntary between 16 and 18 years of age and over 70; compulsory between 18 and 70 years of age.

TIME LINE

IN BRAZIL	IN THE WORLD
	753 B.C. Rome is founded. **116–17 B.C.** Roman Empire reaches its greatest extent under Emperor Trajan (98–17 B.C.). **A.D. 600** Height of Mayan civilization **1000** Chinese perfect gunpowder and begin to use it in warfare.
1494 Treaty of Tordesillas divides the New World between Spain and Portugal, giving the as yet undiscovered area of Brazil to Portugal.	
1530 Coastal Brazil is distributed to Portuguese captains for growing sugarcane.	**1530** Beginning of trans-Atlantic slave trade organized by Portuguese in Africa
1565 Rio de Janeiro is founded.	**1558–1603** Reign of Elizabeth I of England **1620** Pilgrim Fathers sail the Mayflower to America.
1693 Era of gold and diamond mining begins. **1727** Coffee is introduced in Brazil.	
1789 First efforts to establish a republic are crushed.	**1776** U.S. Declaration of Independence **1789–1799** The French Revolution
1807 Napoleon invades Portugal. His son Pedro flees to Brazil. **1815** Brazil is declared a kingdom. **1822** Pedro declares Brazil's independence from Portugal and is crowned Emperor of Brazil. **1831** Pedro I abdicates and leaves the throne to his 5-year-old son, Pedro II. **1841** Pedro II is crowned Emperor.	

IN BRAZIL	IN THE WORLD

1861
U.S. Civil War begins.

1864–70
War of the Triple Alliance;
Argentina, Brazil, and Uruguay fight Paraguay.

1869
The Suez Canal is opened.

1888
The Golden Law abolishes
the practice of owning slaves.

1889
The army deposes Pedro II
and proclaims a republic.

1891
The first Brazilian Constitution is created.

1894
Brazil's first civilian president,
José de Morais Barros, takes office

1914
World War I begins.

1932
São Paolo rebellion results in civil war.

1934
New constitution is adopted; Getúlio Dorneles
Vargas is elected to the presidency.

1937
Estado Novo, or "New State," is established.

1939
World War II begins.

1945
The United States drops atomic bombs on
Hiroshima and Nagasaki.

1949
North Atlantic Treaty Organization (NATO)
is formed.

1957
Russians launch Sputnik.

1964
A military coup puts Marshal Branco in power.

1966–1969
Chinese Cultural Revolution

1985
The military steps down; democracy is restored.

1986
Nuclear power disaster at Chernobyl in Ukraine

1989
The first direct presidential election
since 1960 is held.

1991
Break-up of Soviet Union

1994
The constitution is revised to reduce
the presidential term to four years.

1997
Hong Kong is returned to China.

2001
World population surpasses 6 billion.

GLOSSARY

abraço ("ah-BRAH-soo")
A hug used as a greeting among men.

baiana ("bah-YAH-nah")
Woman from the northern state of Bahia.

bandeirante ("bahn-day-RAHN-teh")
Early explorer of Brazil's interior regions from the state of São Paulo.

beijinhos ("bay-JIN-hoos")
A form of greeting where women kiss other women on the cheek either two or three times.

caboclo ("kah-BOH-cloh")
Brazilian of European and Indian ancestry.

cafuso ("kah-FOO-soh")
Brazilian of African and Indian ancestry.

candomblé ("kahn-dohm-BLEH")
African religion whose adherents believe in the possession of human participants by supernatural spirits.

churrasco ("shoo-HAHS-koo")
Meat roasted on a spit, a popular dish in the south of Brazil.

dendê ("dehn-DAY")
Palm oil used in cooking.

favela ("fah-VEY-lah")
Slum in Brazilian cities.

frevo ("FRAY-voh")
Music and dance style of Northeast Brazil.

futebol ("FOOT-ball")
Soccer, the most popular game in Brazil.

jeito ("JAY-toh")
A way—slang for describing a knack for completing difficult tasks.

macumba ("mah-KOOM-bah")
African religion in which it is believed that the living can communicate with the souls of the dead.

mulatto ("moo-LAH-toh")
Brazilian of European and African ancestry.

orixás ("oh-ree-SHAHS")
African gods brought to Brazil by the slaves.

FURTHER INFORMATION

BOOKS

Benjamin, Medea and Maisa Mendonça. *Benedita da Silva: An Afro-Brazilian Woman's Story of Politics and Love*. California: Food First, 1997.

Burch, Joann Johansen. *Chico Mendes: Defender of the Rain Forest*. Connecticut: Millbrook Press, 1994.

Dawood, Ishie. *Brazil: Land of Contrasts*. Canada: Reidmore Books, 1989.

Gerson, Mary-Joan. *How Night Came From the Sea: A Story From Brazil*. Boston: Little, Brown & Co, 1994.

Lewington, Anna. *Rainforest Amerindians*. Hove, England: Wayland, 1992.

Morrison, Marion. *Brazil*. Country Fact Files series. London: Simon & Schuster, 1993.

WEBSITES

Central Intelligence Agency World Factbook (select "Brazil" from the country list).
www.odci.gov/cia/publications/factbook/index.html

Global Exchange Brazil Campaign. www.globalexchange.org/campaigns/brazil

I Was Born a Black Woman (about the video). www.iwasbornablackwoman.com

Landless Workers Movement. www.mstbrazil.org

Lonely Planet World Guide: Destination Brazil.
www.lonelyplanet.com/destinations/south_america/brazil

Rainforest Action Network. www.ran.org

MUSIC

Brazil: The Essential Album. Manteca, 2000.
Worldbeat Brazil. Green Hill, 2001.

VIDEOS

The Brazil Experience: The Northeast. Lonely Planet, 1995.
I Was Born a Black Woman. Global Exchange, 2000.

BIBLIOGRAPHY

Harrison, Phyllis. *Behaving Brazilian: A Comparison of Brazilian and North American Social Behavior.* Rowley, MA: Newbury House Publishers, 1983.

Taylor, Edwin, ed. *Insight Guides: Brazil.* Singapore: APA Publications, 1989.

Brazilian Embassy in Washington, D.C. Http://www.brasilemb.org/

Greenpeace: Brazil. Http://www.greenpeace.org.br/

Librarwy of Congress Country Studies: Brazil. Http://lcweb2.loc.gov/frd/cs/brtoc.html

United Nations High Commissioner for Refugees (UNHCR) Country Profiles: Brazil. Http://www.unhcr.ch/world/amer/brazil.htm

INDEX